Hoboes

Hoboes

Wandering in America, 1870–1940

RICHARD WORMSER

WALKER AND COMPANY

For Lil and Jack

First published in the United States of America in 1994 by Walker Publishing Company, Inc.

Published simultaneously in Canada by Thomas Allen & Son Canada, Limited, Markham, Ontario

Library of Congress Cataloging-in-Publication Data
Wormser, Richard, 1933–
Hoboes : wandering in America,
1870–1940 / Richard Wormser.
p.   cm.
Includes bibliographical references and index.
ISBN 0-8027-8279-5 (cloth ed.). —ISBN 0-8027-8280-9
(reinforced library ed.)
1. Tramps—United States—History.   2. United States—Social
conditions.   3. Unemployment—United States—History.   4. United
States—Economic conditions.   I. Title.
HV4504.W67   1994
305.5′68—dc20   93-30426
CIP
AC

Photographs not otherwise credited are in the public domain.
Hobo signs on p. 129 adapted from *Knights of the Road: A Hobo History* by Roger Bruns.

Book design by Shelli Rosen

Printed in the United States of America

2   4   6   8   10   9   7   5   3   1

There's a race of men that won't fit in
There's a race that can't stay still.
So they break the hearts of kith and kin
And roam the world at will
They roam the fields and they roam the sea
And they climb the mountain's crest
For theirs is the curse of gypsy blood
And they don't know how to rest.

—ROBERT SERVICE, POET

CONTENTS

■ "Roving Bill" Aspinwall was a professional hobo in the nineteenth century. He was a "mushfakir" — a hobo who roamed the country fixing umbrellas. (*Used by permission of the Antiquarian and Landmark Society, Inc., of Connecticut*)

Introduction

I grabbed a hold of an old freight train
And around the country traveled
And the mysteries of a hobo's life
To me were soon unraveled.

— T - B O N E S L I M , *The Mysteries of a Hobo's Life*

There was a time in America when millions of teenage boys dreamed of becoming hoboes. Nothing seemed more exciting to them than hopping a moving freight train, riding the rods underneath a passenger car, inches away from death, and matching wits with the railroad police. Many young men considered hoboing the ultimate test of manhood. It took courage, toughness, imagination, skill, daring, and strength to live on the road. And though the reality of hobo life was often brutal and tragic, some considered their days on the road the best time of their lives.

The era of the hobo and the tramp lasted for almost eighty years in American life, between the Civil War and the Second World War. The hobo world had its roots in America's rapid industrial growth and the development of the railroad. The hobo was basically a laboring man who wandered the country in search of work. He built railroads, harvested wheat, cut down trees, mined for gold, herded cattle, constructed buildings and bridges—and then moved on. It was his constant wandering that made the hobo a distinct figure.

The hobo world had its own rules, literature, songs, customs, and language. Those who belonged to it usually gave up their real names and identities and took on names of the road such as the Cheyenne Kid, Lord Open Road, Frying Pan Jack, Boxcar Bertha, and Scoop-shovel Scotty. Hoboes wrote songs about themselves; they had their own slang, sign language, and codes of law and honor.

Wanderers appeared early in human history. In medieval days, gypsies, troubadours, and tramp craftsmen traveled through Europe making their living as peddlers and entertainers. They were often accused, sometimes falsely, of stealing and kidnapping children to make beggars out of them. Troubadours were wandering singers who traveled through the countryside, entertaining villages with their songs. The better singers were invited to castles, where they sang for the nobility. Tramp craftsmen were tinkers, cobblers, harness makers, and other artisans who traveled from village to village mending and fixing things. They were welcomed into many homes because not only were they expert repairmen, they were also good company. They were like traveling reporters, filled with information and gossip about the world outside the village. They were known for their humor, songs, and stories.

In America, wandering workers were fairly common by the eighteenth century. There were many complaints about "strangers" suddenly appearing in towns or villages seeking work or public assistance. These "strangers" were part of a small but growing number of wandering poor. Because there were no railroads, most of them traveled fairly near home. The majority were single men seeking work as hired hands on farms. Some were artisans or craftsmen. A few even traveled with their families. A number of women wandered alone from town to town, hoping that someone would either employ them as servants or marry them. If neither happened, they often became charity cases.

Many towns openly discriminated against "strangers," refusing to allow them to enter or even to settle nearby. Local law enforcement officials patrolled the towns at night looking for "night walkers," peo-

■ YOUNG BOYS LEARNED A TRADE EARLY IN LIFE BY WORKING AS APPRENTICES TO AR-
TISANS AND CRAFTSMEN. THEY USUALLY WENT OUT TO WORK ON THEIR OWN AFTER
FIVE TO SEVEN YEARS. MANY OF THEM BECAME WANDERING WORKERS. (*Courtesy of
the Library of Congress*)

ple who, the police believed, did not belong in the area and had no
means of supporting themselves. Such persons were often whipped and
banished from the town or sent to workhouses where they were forced
to work for the community.

One reason people wandered in early America was that the country
was not yet industrially developed. Most people were farmers who
needed some help during the planting and harvesting seasons. There
was also a need for skilled craftsmen who, with their kits of tools, could
build a bed, make a dress, fix a plow, patch a harness, and do a number
of other odd jobs that would earn them at least room and board and
sometimes wages. Many of these floating laborers traveled from town
to town seeking work.

But for the unskilled, the jobs most commonly available were domestic labor for women and farm labor for men. These jobs were not easy to find. In the early days of America, many farm workers and housekeepers were indentured servants. Indenture was a system of servitude in which someone, often an immigrant, contracted to work for an employer for a period of time, usually seven years. In return, the employer paid for the cost of the trip to America, usually from England, and provided room and board. The servant was obligated to pay back the debt by service. At the end of seven years, most servants were free to leave. If they had no place to go, they joined the growing numbers of the homeless traveling from town to town seeking work and shelter from the storms of life.

To some degree, wandering was controlled by the western territories that became available for settlement. Many workers who could not find a job in the more settled coastal regions moved westward to start a new life. The fact that these lands belonged to Native Americans did not bother the settlers. What whites could not gain by treaty, they gained by war. Their technologically superior weapons enabled them to drive the Indians off most of their lands.

Even those wanderers who preferred to continue wandering could make a living off the western land. They hunted and trapped animals, selling their skins and eating their meat. Some became famous pioneers such as Daniel Boone, Kit Carson and Davy Crockett, exploring the wilderness for others to follow. Others became mountain men, who preferred living in the wilderness away from settlers. Mountain men often lived with or near Indians, trapping and hunting animals. Whenever they saw farmers settling nearby, they moved farther west.

Despite the fact that many people were headed west, there were still large numbers of wanderers who remained behind near cities, living from hand to mouth. They were without roots in the community. Like today's homeless, they lived in parks, on riverbanks, and in slums. They were called vagrants. Most were younger men, between twenty

■ ONE OF THE MANY TYPES OF WANDERERS IN EARLY NINETEENTH-CENTURY AMERICA WAS THE MOUNTAIN MAN. MOUNTAIN MEN ROAMED THE MOUNTAINS OF THE WEST TRAPPING AND FISHING, LIVING AMONG INDIANS, AND USUALLY MOVING ON WHEN SETTLERS ARRIVED. (*Courtesy of the Library of Congress*)

and thirty years old, who were unable to read and write. They had poor job skills and no family to support them. Many were like John Kerry, who grew up in Pennsylvania. By the time John was thirteen years old, his father decided he should learn a trade. In those days, children of poor families learned work skills by serving as apprentices to craftsmen. Kerry was apprenticed to a shoemaker. The agreement was that the shoemaker would provide John with room and board and a very small amount of money. In return, John would learn the trade and help the shoemaker with his work.

Many apprentices were extremely ill-treated. They worked hard and long hours, were forced to do other jobs besides the one they were apprenticed to learn, and were poorly fed and sheltered. Most never received any money. At the age of seventeen, Kerry quit his apprenticeship and began to wander about seeking jobs on his own. But there were far more shoemakers than there were jobs for them. Eventually, Kerry ended up in Philadelphia, where he became one of the city's homeless begging for relief.

There were also large numbers of women vagrants in the nineteenth century. Many were widows, or women whose husbands and children had left home to seek work and could not or would not support them. Having lost their families, they had no way to support themselves except as servants. They took to the road in hopes of finding work in people's homes. It was not unusual for a woman to work in a dozen or more homes over a period of several years.

Because there were always more people looking for work than there were jobs, many cities and towns were faced with a growing number of homeless people on the streets. The worst time of year was winter, when it was too cold to live outdoors. Cities and towns usually placed women in poorhouses and other charitable institutions. Men generally applied for relief at the local jail. They were considered criminals. They were kept in a separate area of the jail and given a bed to sleep on and meals at the city's expense. During the spring and summer, these men were thrown out of jail and had to seek farm work.

By 1850, the number of male vagrants in America continued to increase while the number of female vagrants decreased. The main reason was the factory system. Textile factories had been introduced in America, and most factory owners employed women and children because they were cheaper, better workers and less likely to strike than men. Many women who might have been forced to wander could now find employment and even room and board. But these jobs were a mixed blessing. Most factories paid women extremely low wages and

■ THE INTRODUCTION OF THE FACTORY SYSTEM IN AMERICA PROVIDED EMPLOYMENT FOR MANY YOUNG GIRLS SUCH AS THESE WORKERS IN A MATCH FACTORY. WITHOUT FACTORIES, MANY WOMEN WOULD HAVE BECOME WANDERING DOMESTIC WORKERS. *(Courtesy of the Library of Congress)*

■ MANY NORTHERN AND SOUTHERN SOLDIERS, RESTLESS AND SEEKING WORK AND AD-VENTURE, WANDERED THROUGHOUT THE WEST WHEN THE CIVIL WAR ENDED. SOME EVENTUALLY BECAME HOBOES. (*Courtesy of the Library of Congress*)

forced them to work long hours. They were also supervised very closely and could be fired for any reason. Moreover, during hard times, factories would close down and lay off workers. Some would take to the road in search of work.

The Civil War provided work for many men and women, in both the army and civilian life. Railroads were developed and factories built to supply the army. Hundreds of thousands of men were drafted, and as long as the war lasted, there was work—as long as a soldier stayed healthy and alive.

After the Civil War an industrial revolution exploded across America. At its heart was the railroad. Before the war, the United States had 35,000 miles of railroad track. By 1880, it had 93,000 miles; by 1900, 193,000. Every town, city, and state demanded that a railroad pass through its territory. The successful completion of the transcontinental railroad, which linked America from the Atlantic Ocean to the Pacific, led to a construction boom in new lines. Almost two-thirds of railroad construction between 1865 and 1900 was west of the Mississippi River. *The New York Times* observed in the 1880s: "A wilderness is now open to civilization and one which is adequate to support in comfort the surplus population of Europe."

The railroad made it possible for industry to grow. Manufacturers could transport raw materials to a factory and ship finished products out. Farmers and businessmen could raise crops, dig mines, cut lumber, build factories, and carry out thousands of other economic activities because the railroad carried their products to markets. Trains carried more goods farther and faster than any other means of transportation.

Trains also carried hundreds of thousands of workers to fill the jobs the economic boom created. When their jobs ended or there was an economic depression, men and women roamed the country looking for work. These swings between good and hard times produced the hobo. By the end of the nineteenth century, it is estimated, more than a million men were on the road. Most of them were looking for work. The era of the hobo and the tramp was at its height.

■ THE HOBO WAS A WANDERER WHO "FLIPPED" RIDES ON TRAINS TO FIND WORK. (*Courtesy of the Library of Congress*)

1

The "Bindle Stiff": The Hobo Worker

Hobo, hobo . . . where did you come from?
— NINETEENTH-CENTURY CHILDREN'S SONG

"The hobo," wrote Ben Reitman, a Chicago physician who included hoboing among his many talents, "wanders and works. The tramp wanders but does not work and the bum neither wanders nor works." While many on the road saw themselves primarily as wanderers who occasionally worked, hoboes considered themselves primarily workers who wandered to find jobs.

Nobody really knows where the word "hobo" comes from. Some claimed that it came from the Latin *"homo bonus,"* which means good man. Others believed the word is the American version of the French *"hautbois,"* which means oboe but somehow, perhaps through a connection with troubadours, came to describe vagabonds in medieval France. One hobo claimed it came from the greeting "Hello, brother," which was eventually shortened to "hobo." Another theory is that it comes from "hoe-boy"—which is a description of a job on a farm.

Whatever the origins of "hobo," most men who took to the road were hoboes. They were sometimes called "bindle stiffs" because they carried their belongings—usually a shirt and a razor, and sometimes extra clothes—rolled in a "bindle," or blanket, carried on their backs. Hoboes were part of a vast army of migratory labor traveling back and forth in search of jobs. Most were single, under forty, white, and heavy drinkers. Because of this, a large number of them eventually became tramps and bums.

Many of America's first hoboes were ex–Civil War soldiers. They were used to roughing it, had ridden trains, and were made fearless and hardened by the war. A lot of them had no desire to return to the limited opportunities they faced at home. They roamed the country in search of work on the railroads or to find gold and silver or adventure.

Many hoboes were better educated and better trained than earlier generations of wanderers. Ninety percent could read and write. They worked as "boomers," (bridge builders) and "gandy dancers" (railroad men), "bridge snakes" (structural-steel workers on bridges), "skinners" (mule drivers), "timberbeasts" (loggers), and "apple knockers" (apple pickers). Some were carpenters, cigar makers, miners, or printers.

Most of the jobs were temporary. For example, once carpenters completed building a house or a group of houses in a community, they had to move on in search of new work. One carpenter-poet wrote a poem about their experiences, which was published in his union's newspaper:

> Often when a house is built
> Tramping is our luck . . .
> From shop to shop, from town to town
> We often have to go
> 'Tis not all honey in our trade
> I wish you friend to know.

Arthur Vinette, another carpenter, also wrote a letter to his union describing the fate of a carpenter on the road looking for work and competing with his fellow carpenters: "From Ohio to Missouri, tramping over the plain, scaling the snow clad Rockies, as pitiless fate follows in his footsteps. . . . He follows the wide valleys, he is on the line of every railroad, but everywhere there is always a surplus crop of his tribe."

The situation became so bad on the West Coast that the carpenters' union had to warn its members not to travel to California, which many believed was the promised land as far as jobs were concerned. Actually, they would find plenty of hardships there, but little or no work. For every job available, there were five to ten men seeking it.

Miners also had a difficult time finding work. And traveling from job site to job site was especially hard because a miner had to carry his own tools with him. One miner described what he carried as he walked for almost 250 miles between Illinois and Ohio.

> My working tools consist of 13 picks, each nine pounds' weight, besides the "smasher" which weighed twenty-two pounds and has a handle 7 feet long. My sledge hammer is 90 pounds weight and I have four wedges each 2 and ½ feet in length. All my picks were shoved behind my back inside my coat. I carried my sledge over my left shoulder and the wedges in my pockets.

Cigar makers were another group of wandering workers. Their unofficial motto was, "The cigar maker is a wanderer." Almost every young cigar maker was expected to "carry the banner"—that is, live on the road without cash for a while. "I don't know why we did it," one worker said. "Maybe it was the fashion. But you had to take a turn as a hobo."

Unlike many hoboes, cigar makers had little trouble finding work. Cigar making was a highly skilled industry in the nineteenth century. Cigars were made by hand and since many men smoked them (the cigarette had not yet been invented), there were thousands of cigar factories scattered throughout the United States. A skilled worker could usually find a job wherever he roamed. In fact, many factory owners complained that they couldn't keep their skilled laborers long enough. They worked awhile and then went off wandering. In addition, the cigar-makers' union took good care of its members. If a cigar worker arrived in a town, all he had to do to find a place to sleep and eat was introduce himself to the head of the local union. The local would provide him with room and board and try to find him a job. If

■ MINING WAS AMONG
ONE OF THE BETTER-
PAYING JOBS THAT
ATTRACTED HOBOES,
BUT IT WAS ALSO ONE
OF THE MORE DANGER-
OUS. (*Courtesy of the
Library of Congress*)

IMPERIALES,   CONCHAS,   DAMAS,   FABRICA DE TABACOS
REGALIA,   CABALLEROS,   PRENSADOS,
LONDRES,   MILLAR,   PANETELAS,

■ BECAUSE THERE WERE SO MANY CIGAR FACTORIES AROUND THE COUNTRY, MANY
YOUNG MEN "HOBOED" FROM FACTORY TO FACTORY. (*Courtesy of the Library of Congress*)

there was no work, the local would raise enough money for him to
travel to the next village.

Another nineteenth-century wandering worker was the cowboy, a
worker few thought of as a typical hobo. Yet the lives of many cowboys
resembled those of other hoboes. They wandered from job to job. Their
work was often seasonal. In the winter, there was little for them to do.
In the spring and summer, they had to bring the cattle to pasture or
drive them to the cattle markets. One frontier ranch woman laughed
when she was told what Easterners thought about the glamour of the
cowboy. "Shoot—they ain't nothing but farmhands in ten-
gallon hats," she said.

■ Few people think of cowboys as hoboes. Yet, like hoboes, many of them wandered in search of work, riding horses rather than trains. *(Courtesy of the Library of Congress)*

But the true hobo was a man of many trades and talents. He could cut trees, build bridges, repair railroad track, harvest wheat, pick fruit, and drive mules and machines. Some hoboes claimed that their labor built the West, and there is a great deal of truth in this. At certain times of the year, hoboes would suddenly appear in an area like huge flocks of birds. In the Great Plains in July and August for example, freights would be filled with tens of thousands of men arrived to harvest the crops. When there were jobs available, a hobo who had many skills could follow a seasonal cycle of work. The hobo who worked on construction gangs in Ohio in the spring might harvest wheat in Kansas during the summer, plan to work as a longshoreman on the Great Lakes during the fall, and end up in the fruit fields of California in the winter.

Migrant jobs made family life almost impossible. When a married man was on the road, his wife and children suffered. Union newspapers were filled with ads from wives and children seeking information about "the whereabouts of our father." Many of these families were almost destitute. Their ads pleaded, "If any person has knowledge of the whereabouts of my husband and father of our three children, please contact his desperate wife."

During economic depressions, the number of men seeking work dramatically increased. Hundreds of thousands of men lost their jobs. When the economy collapsed in 1873 and again in 1893, it was estimated that over a million men were on the road.

The desperation was so great at times that men would risk their lives for a job. When a ship carrying laborers from the United States to South America sank, drowning all on board, hundreds of unemployed workers in America besieged the shipping office, begging to replace them.

Another worker wrote to his union of the great suffering the depression of 1873 brought to so many workers: "There isn't a damn thing but misfortune to be had. What an ocean of misery. Four million men idle. How many of this vast army are kind fathers, who have homes behind them, a wife and children."

One man described how a depression changed his life for the worse.

I am a vagrant and a vagabond. One year ago I was an industrious, re-spectable head of a family. My family is now a thousand miles away, scattered and broken up. The world is a desert to us. I have no friends, no roof to live under, no table to eat at, no clothes to distinguish me from them. Yet, I am not a thief. I am welcomed by no human being. I am at the mercy of the lowest. Yet I do not feel I could honestly take a pair of shoes or a coat without the owner's consent. What has brought me to this?

Many of these men would never find a stable job again. For them, hoboing became a way of life.

■ ALMOST EVERY HOBO WORKED HARVESTING GRAIN IN THE MIDWEST. HARVEST SEA-SON WAS A TIME WHEN WORK WAS PLENTIFUL AND THE RAILROADS LET HOBOES RIDE FOR FREE WITHOUT BEING THROWN OFF THE TRAINS. (*Courtesy of the Library of Congress*)

■ TRAINS MADE HOBOING POSSIBLE. HOBOES RODE ON, IN, AND UNDER EVERY SECTION OF THE TRAIN, INCLUDING THE PILOT OR FRONT GRID. (*Used by permission of the Antiquarian and Landmark Society, Inc., of Connecticut*)

2

Flipping Freights

I've decked the tops of flying cars
That leaped across the night
The long and level coaches skimmed
Low, like a swallow's flight.

Close to the sleet-bit blinds I've clung
Rocking on and on;
All night I've crouched in empty cars
That rode into the dawn.

— HARRY KEMP, HOBO POET

Without trains, there would not have been hoboes. Traveling was the heart of hobo life, and trains provided the means for travel. In the nineteenth century, the car had not yet been invented and there were only a few roads for wagons and horses. To travel to a job thousands of miles away, the hobo needed transportation. The railroad provided that transportation but to use it the hobo had to learn how to avoid its dangers.

Unlike regular passengers, who paid for their rides, hoboes "flipped" freight trains—that is, they jumped on board without paying. Hoboes rode almost every freight train that moved in the West despite the fact that the railroad hired guards to catch them. They rode inside freight cars, underneath them, on the top, front, rear, and sides.

While a few specialized in passenger trains, which were far more difficult and dangerous to ride, most hoboes preferred freights. An experienced hobo knew every different kind of freight car and the best place
to ride in each of them. They traveled in the gondolas (open cars), the
"side-door" Pullmans, boxcars (closed cars), and reefers (refrigerator
cars). To escape detection, they would hide themselves in the coal of
coal cars and among cattle in cattle cars. Riding a train almost became
an art form. A hobo's life depended upon knowing how to correctly
board a train and ride on it, in or under it. And, most important, he
needed to know how to avoid being caught.

The easiest way to board a freight train was to sneak into a boxcar
before it left the yard. But hoboes who boarded this way were usually
caught. The railroad yards were filled with "shacks" (brakemen) and
"railroad dicks" or "railroad bulls" (railroad police), who were continually searching for hoboes.

Many hoboes preferred to board a train as it was slowly pulling out
of the yard. Before the train left, they would hide underneath rail ties,
behind trees, and under bridges waiting for the "shack" to give the
locomotive engineer the "highball" sign (the signal to start). Then, as
the train started forward, they dashed out of their hiding places and
ran alongside the train. An experienced hobo always chose the spot
where he wanted to board beforehand. He would run alongside the
train until the car he wanted was next to him. Then he would run at
full speed and grab hold of a ladder, a bar, or any part of the car that
provided enough leverage to swing aboard. Tom Kromer in *Waiting for
Nothing* described boarding a train as follows:

> I judge my distance, I start running along this track, I hold my hand up
> to the side of the cars. I feel this step hit my fingers. . . . I grab it as tight
> as I can. I think my arms will be jerked out of their sockets. My ribs feel
> like they are smashed. I hang on. I make it.

Willie Davis was one hobo who *didn't* make it. In his *Autobiography
of a Super Tramp*, he wrote:

■ The bumpers were a comfortable spot for hoboes to ride but they could be spotted easily there. *(Courtesy of the Library of Congress)*

Taking a firm grip on the bar, I jumped but it was too late as the train was now going at a rapid rate. My foot came short of the step and I fell and still clinging to the handle bar, was dragged several yards before I relinquished my hold. And there I lay for several minutes . . . while the train swiftly passed in the darkness. I attempted to stand but found that something happened to prevent me from doing this. Sitting in an upright position, I then began to examine myself and now found that the right foot was severed below the ankle.

Even after a hobo had climbed aboard, he was still not safe. He had to find a place to rest that provided comfort and security from the crew. The most comfortable place was usually an empty boxcar. It protected riders from bad weather, and if there was straw on the floor a hobo could make a soft bed and keep himself warm.

But boxcars were vulnerable. Not only could a hobo be easily caught, but there were also many physical dangers hoboes had to face once the train was under way. They might be thrown out of cars at high speeds if the boxcar doors opened without warning. Or a hobo could be decapitated if the doors suddenly closed as he was standing in the doorway. Some were crushed when the cargo in a loaded boxcar they were riding suddenly shifted position. Still, for all the dangers, many hoboes preferred riding boxcars because of their comfort and protection against bad weather.

In hot weather, some hoboes liked to ride in "reefer" (refrigerated) cars. The problem was that reefers were locked from the outside. A number of hoboes froze to death inside reefers because yardmen un-knowingly—or sometimes knowingly—locked the car with men inside.

The blinds was one of the favorite spots of those who rode the passenger trains. Sometimes called "blind baggage," the blinds was the front platform of the baggage car or mail car of passenger trains, be-tween the engine and the first car. It was a relatively safe place to ride, because the door leading to the platform was not used since baggage was piled up against it. But hoboes who rode there had to swallow a lot of dust and ashes thrown up from the front of the train. It was hard to catch someone riding the blinds as long as the train was moving. But once the train stopped, the blinds was the first place detectives looked for hoboes.

Some hoboes preferred riding the bumpers, the small platforms between cars. They were exposed to bad weather, but if they were spotted, at least they had a chance of getting off and escaping. Hoboes also "decked rattlers" (rode the top of a freight car) if the weather was good and the roof was relatively flat. But in case of rain, snow, or cold, the ride could become a nightmare.

"Roving Bill" Aspinwall recalled riding on top of a mail car during a storm:

> The rain splattered on the roof like broken pearls. A wind whirled over the train. The lightning flared again. I started to crawl from under the windswept rain. I slipped and grabbed the pipe as the train swerved. I lay still. The wind lashed through my shirt with the sting of a rawhide whip while I lay face downwards, and held to the small pipe with aching hands. Choosing rather to be lashed by the rain than to crawl across the wet and speeding train I made no move. . . . Silently I fought with a primitive lust for life. I pounded the roof of the car to revive the ebbing circulation of my blood. I slapped my forehead with a free hand. I thought of the lad who had been riding the top when the train speeded under a low bridge. It threw him far from the train with a crushed skull, into the last oblivion that comes to tramp and king.

There was no part of a train that an enterprising hobo would not try to convert into a hiding place. A few even tried stuffing themselves in the battery boxes that were located underneath passenger coaches. One hobo named Frisco described how his ride almost cost him his life:

> The door flopped open and the wind came on me ice-cold and yelpin' like a pack of dogs. The limited was hitting her up to fifty miles an hour. The door slammed up and down and I thought every second she'd stroke a high tie and rip the old battery box with me right out from under the

■ Jack London, the famous writer, reenacts how he "decked" a passenger train—that is, rode on the top. Decking was extremely dangerous because the rider could be blown off by winds and was at the mercy of bad weather. (*Courtesy of the Library of Congress*)

car and send us smashing to hell. Holy smokes, I was scairt. Then the train hit a curve so fast I had to fight like a whitehead [a kind of fresh-water fish] to keep her from pitching me out. I was paddling and clawing with both hands and feet like a mouse on a treadmill. . . . By and by the door flew shut. And I hung on to her most of the night just like a guy that's trying to hold on to a bull calf that's ripping and roaring.

The hardest test for hoboes was "riding the rods." The rod was a four-foot-long bar underneath the four-wheel truck of a passenger car. Of all the bars underneath the carriage of a train, it was the hardest and most dangerous to reach. Many hoboes considered riding the rods to be the true test of a " 'bo." The rider had to reach beneath the railway car as the train was picking up speed, swing himself under-neath, and then crawl until he reached the rods. Then he took out his "ticket" (a thick pine board about a foot and a half long, with a groove cut in it) and slipped the groove over the rod and made a seat for himself. As long as a hobo sat there, he could not be seen. But he was still in danger. Beneath him were the cinder and tracks of the railroad. One slip and he was finished. In the period between 1901 and 1905 alone, the railroads reported that almost 25,000 hoboes had been killed or seriously injured by trains on which they were riding. Josiah Flynt, a nineteenth-century hobo-turned-writer, in his book *Tramping with Tramps* described the death of Boston Mary, a woman hobo who rode the rails. Boston Mary was drunk but insisted on riding the rods of the "flying mail" train out of Boston, a high-speed express train. Mary and her companion boarded underneath the train and sat on the rods. At first everything went well. But as the train picked up speed, both had to hold on for their lives as the train threw up dirt and rocks at them. Boston Mary's hair began to blow into the eyes of her com-panion and he could not see to help her:

The way the wind and the gravel 'n the dust flew round our faces 'n the cramps that took us settin so crooked like, was enough to make bigger blokes give up. And to make things worse, her hair was blowin all over my face 'n I could hardly see. . . . Old Mary got to swearing. "The flying

■ THE MOST DANGEROUS
PLACE TO RIDE ON A
TRAIN WAS ON THE
RODS UNDERNEATH
THE TRAIN. ONE SLIP
AND THE WHEELS
CRUSHED YOU.
*(Used by permission
of the Antiquarian
and Landmark Society,
Inc., of Connecticut)*

mail, oh I say, the flying mail." I called out every few minutes to keep her calm. . . . She was doing her best. She was getting wilder every minute and when her old hair had stopped swirling and me eyes were free again, I was hangin on alone and the wheels carried me far away from where the old girl was lying.

Another danger in riding underneath the car was that a hobo was vulnerable to bulls or shacks lowering a piece of iron on a rope between cars. When the iron reached the tracks, the brakeman could maneuver it underneath the car by letting out the rope. Once underneath the car, the iron bar became a deadly weapon. The speed of the train would make the bar swing like a pendulum, destroying everything it came in contact with. It smashed rods and riders alike and any hobo who was struck by the bouncing iron would be either killed outright or knocked to the tracks where the train would run over him. The only way to safety was to try and jump out from underneath the train far enough to clear it.

There was a constant battle of wits between the bulls and hoboes. Railroad police hated hoboes not only because they rode trains without paying, but also because they damaged railroad cars and their contents. If the weather was cold, hoboes might start a fire inside a boxcar, which sometimes got out of control and burned the car. At times, they would distract the crew by deliberately setting fire to a boxcar, and then steal the merchandise in another car.

Sometimes bulls and shacks would try to shake hoboes down for money, making them pay anywhere from fifty cents to a few dollars to ride. Many hoboes paid rather than be "ditched" (thrown off the train). A few, however, refused. When asked for money, Bill Tully, a hobo, proudly replied, "I wouldn't give you a cut if you gave me a Pullman berth. It's against my principles."

If a hobo was caught, the best he could hope for was that he would only be ditched. But a number of railroad bulls enjoyed beating up on hoboes they caught. One bull had a mean reputation for carrying a

■ It was the job of the brakeman and/or "shack" (railroad cop) to prevent hoboes from riding the trains. *(Courtesy of the Library of Congress)*

metal dog chain that he smashed on the heads or backs of hoboes he caught riding trains on his line. Some railroad bulls tossed hoboes off moving trains or beat them with "saps" (blackjacks) or fists. One railroad cop named Hotchkiss described his methods in the 1890s when he caught a hobo in his yard:

> I'd go and ask a guy a question. I'd cuff him across the face with a good slap. If you were getting the hell out'a there, I'd give him the billy, not hard enough to break anything but hard enough so he'd remember.

Ethel Lynn, a woman who hoboed across the country during the depression of 1907, recalled in her *Adventures of a Woman Hobo* seeing what happened to a hobo caught on a train by a detective: "I saw a hobo make a running leap into a gondola. The detective leaped in beside the hobo who scrambled madly up the end of the boxcar ahead. . . . The two men reached the roof almost together. The detective made a mighty swing with his billy at the hobo's head. There was a crack like a revolver shot and the hobo pitched from the top of the rapidly moving car and rolled head over heels down the embankment."

Some bulls were killers. One man feared by all hoboes was Jeff Carr, a notorious railroad dick who patrolled the railroad yards in Cheyenne, Wyoming. Carr enjoyed riding alongside a slow-moving freight and shooting hoboes who were riding the blinds or decking the top. Those he didn't shoot, he would throw underneath the wheels. Sometimes he took wounded hoboes to cells and left them to die without treatment. Carr was finally clubbed to death in a fight with two hoboes.

To many young men, the dangers of riding the train were part of the appeal and the adventure. One young hobo wrote:

> I was part of the road, not a hero but a youth bewildered, unwanted, running along swaying catwalks of fast moving trains, and jumping from car to car, opening the doors of empty refrigerator cars in the yards and perilously swinging into them as the train hit 50. Occasionally

flying onto a great "high balling train"—riding in the blind baggage of passengers and choking in everlasting dust, hearing the shriek of the rider whose foot was caught between the coupling pin when the train bucked.

They were proud of their skills and of their ability to survive. But there were other dangers that many hoboes feared far more than riding the rails. One of these was the tramp, who could be the worst danger of all.

■ THIS IS A GROUP PORTRAIT OF "PROFESHES," TRAMPS WHO TOOK PRIDE IN THEIR DRESS AND THEIR WAY OF LIFE. THE PICTURE WAS TAKEN AT THE REQUEST OF A COLLEGE PROFESSOR STUDYING TRAMP LIFE. (*Used by permission of the Antiquarian and Landmark Society, Inc., of Connecticut*)

3

"Vampires" of the Road: Tramps

Tramp, tramp, tramp keep on trampin
Nothin doin here for you
If I catch you round again
You will wear the ball and chain
Keep on trampin that's the best thing you can do.

— TRADITIONAL HOBO VERSE

Many hoboes feared tramps as much as or more than they feared the police. Like the hobo, the tramp was a wanderer. But he was not a worker. Most tramps lived by their wits, most by petty thievery and begging, some by robbery and murder. The hobo was contemptuous of the tramp as a loafer, while the tramp despised the hobo as a sucker for working.

The distinction between tramps and hoboes, however, was not always clear-cut. Many men on the road lived in both worlds, hoboing to make a "stake" (earn some money), then living without working until the stake ran out. Some hoboes eventually became tramps, especially when there was no work to be found, and some tramps became hoboes. But even though tramps and hoboes often lived in different worlds as far as work was concerned, they shared the same space. Hoboes and tramps flipped the same trains, ate and slept in the same jungles, and were locked up in the same jail cells.

The tramp world had its own society, with its own rules and its own hierarchy. At the top of the list was the "profesh," or professional. The "profesh" was often distinguished by his good clothes, his personal neatness, and the fact that he frequently slept on newspapers. Some tramps were criminals and had bad reputations as killers and thieves. Others were con men who cheated people out of their money. The aristocrats of the profesh were "yeggs" (safecrackers). They robbed "obeys" (post offices) and "jugs" (banks). A yegg "blew" (blew open) a "pete" (safe) with "soup" (nitroglycerin).

Sometimes tramp criminals traveled together in "pushes" (gangs). Hoboes called pushes "vampires of the road" and feared them. Many were vicious and preyed on hoboes and migrant workers, as well as on boys and young men new to the road. Pushes often rode the freight trains looking for victims to rob and murder. They would travel in areas where they knew hoboes had recently been paid off after a season's work. A hobo was lucky if they only robbed him. Sometimes pushes threw their victims off fast-moving trains or tossed them between the wheels.

Another type of tramp was the fakir. Fakirs were often part con man, part repairman. The best known of these was the mushfakir, who was an umbrella mender. Sometimes the umbrella and the mushfakir would disappear together. Some fakirs sharpened scissors and knives. Many of them really were skilled repairmen, but they preferred to wander as they worked and work when they felt like it.

Tramps often developed a "front" to con people out of money. Almost every young tramp had a story about a sick brother, a dying mother, or the need to get to the next town, where a job was waiting. Some panhandled by pretending they had deformities and diseases. Tramps who pretended they were blind were called "blinks," while others, called "deafies" and "dummies," pretended they were deaf and mute. Tramps who faked cerebral palsy or another muscle-control disease were called "floppers." "Ghosts" were men falsely claiming to be tubercular. Some men could distort their bodies in such a way as to appear not to have hands. They were known as "hand-hiders."

Most tramps lived by "battering the stem"—begging on the main street or in other public places. Almost every day, tramps wandered through cities, towns, and farm areas, asking for handouts. They would often spend the whole day knocking on the doors of houses asking for something to eat or wear. Some tramps went to extreme means to attract attention. One ate grass in front of a house to demonstrate how hungry he was.

To survive, a tramp had to know whom to approach and how to approach them. One tramp drew up a begging rulebook in which he advised that the groups of people most sympathetic to beggars were workers, married women, prostitutes, and nuns. Wealthy men and ministers were to be avoided. One tramp noted that "Catholic sisters are good marks; all of them, if sometimes gloomy, are at least good-natured to the needy." The most successful tramps were those who knew how to invent a good story. In *Jack London: On the Road*, London, who was a marvelous storyteller and eventually became one of America's best-known writers, described the technique:

> First of all, the beggar must size up his victim. After that, he must tell a good story that will appeal to the peculiar personality and temperament of that particular victim. And here come the great difficulty. Not a minute is allowed for preparation. As in a lightning flash, he must divine the nature of his victim and conceive a tale that will hit home.

London keenly saw how the poor were far more generous than the rich.

> The poor constitute the last resource of the hungry tramp. The poor can always be depended upon. They give, they withhold never from what they need for themselves. A bone to the dog is not charity. Charity is the bone shared with the dog when you are just as hungry as the dog.

When begging didn't work, tramps stole food. They became experts at stealing chickens from henhouses, fruit from orchards,

■ THE "JUNGLE" WAS
THE HOBO/TRAMP
COMMUNITY CENTER.
HERE HOBOES ATE,
SLEPT, AND RELAXED.
EVERYONE BROUGHT
SOMETHING TO SHARE
IN THE COMMON
MEAL. *(Used by
permission of the
Antiquarian and
Landmark Society, Inc.,
of Connecticut)*

■ THE WRITER JACK LONDON SPENT PART OF HIS TEENAGE YEARS AS A HOBO. (*Co*
of the Library of Congress)

vegetables from grocery trucks, and milk from doorsteps.

The common meeting ground of tramps and hoboes was the "jun-gle." The jungle was a campsite, usually located outside of town near the railroad tracks. Jungles were also located near a water supply. Despite the common belief that tramps hated to wash, most took great pride in personal cleanliness and neatness. Many carried a razor, or a piece of broken glass with which they shaved. They washed their clothes, took baths in the river, and hung their clothes to dry on branches. They mended their socks and tried to keep at least some of their clothes as neat as possible.

In some communities, the police did not bother the inhabitants of the jungle as long as it was quiet. However, no jungle was ever completely safe from harassment. Even the most peaceful jungles were raided from time to time—especially if a crime had been committed in the area.

The jungle was like a community center in which everybody was welcome as long as they obeyed the rules. There was seldom racial or ethnic discrimination. But while blacks and Hispanics were usually welcome, racial battles did erupt at times as there were some individual tramps with strong racial prejudices.

In the jungle, there was food, a place to sleep, and companionship. The main event of the day was dinner. As one tramp noted, "The tramp is the hungriest person in the world. No matter who he is, his appetite is usually ravenous." Both hoboes and tramps lived in a state of constant hunger; rarely did anyone ever get enough food to satisfy him. The main meal, generally served in the evening, was usually a large stew called a Mulligan stew. It contained mostly vegetables, unless somebody was lucky enough to be given or have stolen a "gump" (chicken) or piece of meat. To share in the meal one had to contribute. Those who did not bring food had to work as chefs or gather firewood, unless they were ill.

Everyone in the jungle was expected to contribute his share to the general supply of either food, liquor, or money. He had to find firewood and to clean his pots and dishes after he finished eating. It was forbidden to rob other men in the jungle while they slept, or to light fires that might attract the attention of the police. Any violation of these rules could lead to a tramp being thrown out by force.

After dinner, men would often sit around a fire and tell stories about the adventures they had, the fast trains they had ridden, and the jails they had been in. They talked about policemen and judges to be avoided and bragged about fights they had fought (and won). They told others which towns were friendly and which were hostile. Some men would get into deep social and political discussions. Many tramps and hoboes were self-educated and widely read in economics and political philosophy. Many hoboes were familiar with Karl Marx and were deeply influenced by socialism and revolutionary theory.

Hoboes and tramps often sang songs and recited poetry in a jungle gathering. There was a rich tradition of songs and poetry in the hobo/tramp world. Many hoboes knew the poems of Kipling and Tennyson by heart. Harry Kemp, probably the most famous of the hobo poets, always carried a volume of Keats's poems with him when he traveled.

Sooner or later, the conversation would turn to women. Any man who could tell entertaining stories about women was sure to find an audience. But in reality, few tramps had relationships with women other than prostitutes. Part of the reason that many men were on the road was that they could not sustain relationships with women. This was not as true of the hobo, who sometimes had a family and had to travel from job to job to support them. But the hobo and tramp world was primarily male, and homosexuality was common. Even among the few women hoboes, there were some women who were lovers and traveled together, avoiding men whenever possible.

If times were bad and there was little or no food to be had, tramps and hoboes turned to public assistance or the mission houses run by ministers. The best-known mission was the "Sallies"—the Salvation Army. There were a number of smaller missions, most of which were less interested in providing food and shelter than in converting men to their form of Christianity. Any hobo who accepted mission hospitality had to listen to a sermon that might last for hours, and perform hard work in addition. The food was usually pretty bad—bologna sandwiches or beans and stew. Many complained that the meat in the sandwich was thin enough to see through and that the piece of meat in the stew was small enough to hide behind a single bean.

One popular song expressing the hypocrisy of many missionaries was Joe Hill's ballad "The Preacher and the Slave," which contained the following lines:

Long-haired preachers come out tonight.
Try to tell you what's wrong and what's right
But when you ask for something to eat
They will answer you in voices so sweet.

You will eat bye and bye,
In that glorious land in the sky;
Work and pray, live on hay
You'll get pie in the sky when you die.

■ WHEN IT WAS DIFFICULT TO GET A HANDOUT, MANY HOBOES AND TRAMPS WENT TO A MISSION, WHERE THEY COULD GET A MEAL—BUT ONLY AFTER LISTENING TO SEV-ERAL HOURS OF BORING SERMONS. (*Used by permission of the Antiquarian and Landmark Society, Inc., of Connecticut*)

Tramps might mock missionaries, but they were very respectful about religion. They saw Jesus Christ as a wanderer like themselves, and referred to him as "Jerusalem Slim." One of the favorite biblical passages of some men on the road was "The foxes have holes, and the birds of the air have nests; but the Son of Man hath not where to lay his head." And a popular hobo poem of the time contained the lines:

> *You call me Christ Jesus with intelligence slim*
> *But I was a rebel called Jerusalem Slim*
> *And my brother: the outcast, the rebel the tramp*
> *And not the religious, the scab or the scamp.*

The last resort of tramps and hoboes for food and lodging was jail. In some towns, sheriffs would allow a tramp to stay in jail for the night, feeding him dinner and breakfast before turning him loose. Sometimes, a request could backfire: Some tramps were kept in jail, serving as much as six months at hard labor on a vagrancy charge. But during depressions a number of local sheriffs were willing to keep them on a short-term basis. One advantage for the sheriff was that a tramp in jail was less likely to steal some farmer's chicken.

Despite the fact that many hoboes and tramps were constantly on the road and had no access to telephones, telegraphs, or the mails, they developed a complex system of communication. By arranging rocks in a certain way, a tramp could leave a message for those who came after him that a certain house was a good or bad place to ask for a handout. There was also a system of signs used to let tramps know where they might find a friendly or hostile reception. Directions to a welcoming place might be indicated by drawing a chalk circle on a tree or stone, with a line to the right or left indicating the direction in which to turn. A sketch of a comb, with its teeth, might mean "Beware a dog who bites tramps." Men also wrote messages for each other on water tanks along railroad tracks. They wrote their name, destination, and the date, with an arrow pointing in the direction they were head-

■ HOBOES WHO WERE TAKEN TO THE HOSPITAL FEARED THEY WOULD BE GIVEN THE "BLACK BOTTLE," WHICH MANY BELIEVED CONTAINED POISON TO KILL THOSE WHO WERE POOR AND SICK.

ing. Any of their friends who saw the message knew when they had been there and where to find them.

If a tramp got sick, the last place he wanted to go was the county hospital. There was a firm belief among tramps that doctors and nurses would make them drink from a mysterious "Black Bottle" which would kill them. In his book, *Beggars of Life*, Jim Tully, a hobo author, explained this fear:

> The Black Bottle contained some deadly poison. In the silence of the night, the sick and wasted one was given a spoonful of it and the bed was made ready for another patient. . . . Granted this may be nearly all superstition, yet its root may be planted in fact. At any rate, all vagrants believed it. . . . I feared not death at this time. I did fear the Black Bottle.

■ HOBOES AND TRAMPS
SLEPT WHERE THEY
COULD, SOMETIMES
EVEN ON THE FLOOR
OF A POLICE STATION.
*(Used by permission of
the Antiquarian and
Landmark Society, Inc.,
of Connecticut)*

Most tramps stayed on the road until they died or were killed. They died under the wheels of trains, in knife fights with fellow tramps, or at the hands of the police. Some froze to death inside boxcars or died of consumption and pneumonia in jungles and flophouses.

Yet despite its harshness, life on the road had a sometimes over-whelming attraction for teenage boys throughout America. Hundreds of thousands of them took to the road. For some, it was the worst mistake of their life.

4

Road Kids

Granddad I want to be a hobo
That's what I want to do
Help me if you can, when I get to be a man
I want to be a hobo too.

— TRADITIONAL HOBO VERSE

On a hot summer's day in 1891, fifteen-year-old Jack London went for a swim in the Sacramento River in California, where he met a rough bunch of teenagers. London was as tough as any of them. He had already been the leader of a San Francisco band of oyster pirates, thieves who raided the oyster beds of commercial fishermen. London had been in many fights, seen men killed, and come close to death himself. Besides being an oyster pirate, he had sold newspapers on the streets, labored in a factory sixty hours a week for ten cents an hour, and shoveled coal thirteen hours a day for eight cents an hour.

London soon discovered that he had fallen in with a group of road kids, wild youths who tramped around the country looking for excitement. The language they spoke was a language he had never heard before. In his book *The Road*, London recorded it. One example: "Da stem? Nit. Yaeggin on the sugar train. Hit a fly on the main drag for a light piece and the bull snatched me got a t'ree hour blin." ("On the main avenue, I begged a plainclothes cop for a small stake and he arrested me and the judge gave me three hours to leave town.")

The road kids invited London to join their "push," or gang. London didn't hesitate. They were a wild bunch, fiercely loyal to each other and a terror to those they preyed upon. They taught Jack to make a living by "jackrolling" (robbing drunks and bindle stiffs) and by stealing from the local Chinese. They showed him how to "batter the stem." They even gave him a road name, "The Sailor Kid." London quickly and enthusiastically joined the gang. But although he was a good pupil and a willing fighter—even going to jail for three days for brawling in the street—he was not yet a road kid. He would remain a "gay cat," or tenderfoot, until he passed his test: riding the blinds on an express train across the Sierra Nevada mountains.

On the night of his initiation, Jack was joined by another teenager, "The French Kid," who was also being initiated. The two teenagers crouched in the darkness near the yard from which the train would depart. When they heard its slow chugging and saw its bright light, they crouched and waited until the engine passed. Then they ran to jump aboard before the train picked up speed. Jack "nailed the blinds"—swung on board the mail car. The French Kid then grabbed the rail to pull himself on board. Suddenly he slipped, and before Jack could reach out and grab him, The French Kid fell between the cars and onto the rails. He lived, but lost both his legs.

Once on the train, Jack "decked her"—he climbed onto the roof of the train. He had been warned to do so because the train passed a town where there was a "horstyle" (hostile) bull who searched the train for hoboes. After the train was safely by, Jack had to slide down to the blind baggage to pass his test.

But sliding down from the top of a train to a small space between the cars while the train is moving at fifty miles an hour is not an easy thing to do, especially for a fifteen-year-old who has never done it before and has no one to help him. So, freezing half to death, Jack remained holding on to the deck as the train sped over the snow-covered mountains and roared through tunnels in the bitter cold. He never told any of the push that he had not ridden the blinds. As far as they were concerned, he had passed the test. He was now a road kid.

■ A SMALL NUMBER OF
TRAMPS CALLED "JOCKERS"
TRIED TO SEDUCE YOUNG
BOYS TO JOIN THEM ON
THE ROAD.

Jack eventually became a "profesh" and was able to ride in every
section of the train. Although he traveled on the road on and off for
several years, he never forgot the feelings he had riding the trains at
night:

> I lay on my back with a newspaper under my back for a pillow. Above
> me the stars were winking and wheeling in squadrons back and forth as
> the train rounded curves, and watching them, I fell asleep. The day was
> done—one day of all my days. Tomorrow would be another day and I was
> young.

Jack London was one of thousands of road kids looking for excitement, adventure, and work in the Far West. It was a time when the West was opening and railroads were connecting the country. The illusion of freedom had great appeal to young men. They believed a life on the road would free them from the tyranny of abusive parents and teachers and a lifetime of dull and menial factory work. Jim Tully was a teenager working for a few dollars a week in a factory in St. Marys, Ohio, who hated every minute of his job. One day, a road kid passing through town told him, "Only boobs work. Them old whistles blow every morning and they piles out like a lot of cattle." It was a perfect description of Tully's existence, as he wrote in *Beggars of Life*:

> The horror of the town and my life crept over me. The factory whistles every morning, calling men to labor, had always grated on my nerves like files on glass. I saw the many men hurrying to work carrying battered dinner buckets. . . . I thought of my life during all the months—working for three dollars a week and paying two dollars for board.

Two weeks later he was on the road: "I was going somewhere. Over to the next valley were life and dreams and hope. Monotony and the wretched routines of a drab Ohio town would be unknown. I was at last on the road to high adventure."

Tully, like many road kids, was raised in poverty. Most were children of working-class families. Many were raised by one parent or, like Tully, were orphans. They were at the bottom of the social ladder. Pretty girls and popular athletes would have nothing to do with them. Tully dreamed of making his fortune and then returning to town in triumph.

> I would show the aristocratic girls who snubbed me on Main Street that I was not what they thought I was. I would not come back until everybody heard of me—and when I did come back people would say, "There goes Jimmy Tully, he used to be a little drunkard and look at him now—shows what a fellow can do in this country if he works hard and saves his money."

■ ROAD KIDS WERE
ALWAYS VULNERABLE
WHEN THEY TRAVELED
ALONE.

Once on the road, the hobo left his past life behind him. One hobo wrote: "When I was pulled through the door of a boxcar, I was pulled into another world. . . . I felt that my past life had been shut out. I was no longer a plodding farmhand. I had stepped outside the law [to] where men live by their wits."

For some of the young men who had families, departure meant severing all ties. Many hoboes and tramps would never see their parents again. An old hobo ballad, "Where Is My Wandering Brat Tonight?"

expressed this tragedy. The poem contrasts a mother at home worrying about her son, who has run away to become a hobo, with an old hobo brutally telling her what is happening to her boy on the road.

Where is my wandering boy tonight?
The boy of his mother's pride.
Oh, he's counting the ties with a bed on his back
Or else he is dinging a ride
He's on the head of a cattle train, lady
That's where y're brat is tonight.

His heart may be pure as the morning dew
But his togs are a sight to see
If he's nailed for a vag [vagrant], his plea won't do.
"Sixty days," said the judge, "you see."
Oh, where is my boy tonight?
Oh, where is my boy tonight?
The chilly wind blows, to the hoosegow he goes
That's where your brat is tonight.

The first anxious moment that a gay cat had to pass was meeting other tramps and hoboes. In *Beggars of Life*, Jim Tully described how, at the end of his first ride on a train, he dropped off in town on a cold and snowy night. Looking for a place to warm himself, he saw an old shed at the end of the tracks. As he approached it, he could hear the murmur of voices. The shed was filled with hoboes and tramps. Tully was nervous, but he opened the door and walked on. Everyone stopped talking for a moment and looked at him. Then one man acknowledged him with the traditional greeting of the road, "Hello Bo."

Once he was seated, no one paid attention to him; the conversation continued. Tully fearfully looked the men over as he listened to the conversation. One man's mouth sagged at one corner where a red scar led downward as though a knife had cut it. The men spoke about trains they had ridden and places they had been. They talked of hoboes they all knew, some of whom had died. They warned each other about places and towns hostile to hoboes.

As Tully listened to the most fascinating conversation he had ever heard, one of the men offered him some food and coffee. As Tully wolfed down his dinner, one of the tramps gave him some advice: "You ain't been on the road long kid. It takes a lot of guts for a green kid to beat it on a day like this. If I was you, I'd beat it back home until the bluebirds whistle in the spring."

Before Tully could think over the advice, the door to the shack was suddenly thrown wide open and a police officer walked in. But instead of arresting everybody, he told them to relax and shared a cup of coffee with them. "It's too cold to be outside." Later, when the policeman left, the hoboes talked about what a good guy he was. One old tramp shook his head and said you couldn't trust any cop. He was right. A few hours later, as the men were sleeping, the officer returned with his partner. Both had their guns drawn. They lined everybody up and took them down to the police station. It seemed that a robbery had been committed and the hoboes were naturally the first suspects. Tully was scared he would be sent to jail, as the police officer made him try to confess to the crime or at least tell who had committed it. But the policemen believed his story that he was "green" and let him go.

The police were only one of the many dangers facing a green road kid. For many, the worst threat of all was the "wolf" or "jocker," the tramp who preyed on "lambs" (inexperienced young men). Josiah Flynt observed how many of them operated: "When you see a trainload of tramps, there is always a 'wolf' on the tender. Like vultures following a caravan, these perverts trail boys, waiting to ensnare them. These men become friendly with a lonely boy and try to seduce him."

The jocker was usually an older tramp who had a great deal of experience on the road. He often approached young men, offering to show them the ropes. Eventually a sexual relationship would develop. The youth would become the jocker's "punk."

Punks were often held in slavery by their jockers. Sometimes jockers would give them feminine names such as "Mabel," "Sally," or "my sweetie pie." The punk would be forced to wash the jocker's

■ SOMETIMES A YOUNG MAN WAS FORCED TO TRAVEL WITH OLDER TRAMPS; OTHER TIMES, HE JOINED THEM WILLINGLY FOR PROTECTION. *(Courtesy of the Library of Congress)*

clothes, shave him, cook his meals, and beg for money and food.

While jockers were occasionally accused of kidnapping children, more often they seduced them to run away on the road. They usually picked the children of the poor because few poor people had the means to pursue the jocker, even if they wanted to. In most cases, the police assumed the boy had run away from an unhappy home. Josiah Flynt, a hobo at the end of the nineteenth century, described the jocker's approach as follows: "He stops at a town for a few hours, collects a group of boys at his hangout, picks out the one who will serve him best and then begins to systematically fascinate him."

The jockers would tell boys about the fun and adventure they would have on the road. Believing this, many youths, especially those who were unhappy at home, followed them. Once on the road, they quickly learned to do what was expected of them if they wanted to survive.

One way a teenager on the road could protect himself from jockers was to fight, or at least let the jocker know he would. When Jim Tully met a tramp who asked him point-blank, "You ever had a jocker? You're a pretty smart looking boy," Tully immediately replied: "I'd bust a jocker on the nose that'd try to make me out a sucker." The tramp backed off and let Tully alone.

Josiah Flynt noticed that the worst jockers were usually those who had once been punks themselves: "I know of no roadster so cruel or mean to the weak or young fellow. This is not surprising however when one realizes that for years he has been subjected to the whims and passions of various jockers and that he is only able to wreak his feelings on the nearest victim."

Besides fighting, another way a road kid could protect himself was to team up with someone his own age who had more experience on the road. Most jockers steered clear of road kids who traveled together, for they were generally more vicious and relentless in a fight. They valued their freedom and would fight harder for it.

Tully found such a traveling companion in Bill, an orphan who had spent five years in reform school. Bill swore that he would die before going back to prison. Shortly after Tully teamed up with him, they hopped a mail train, where a detective posing as a hobo arrested and handcuffed them together. Both were certain to be sent to jail. Bill said nothing but waited until the detective was distracted for a moment and turned his back to them. Suddenly Bill moved toward him and gave him a kick, sending him flying out of the moving boxcar. Later on, Tully and Bill jumped off the train while still handcuffed together.

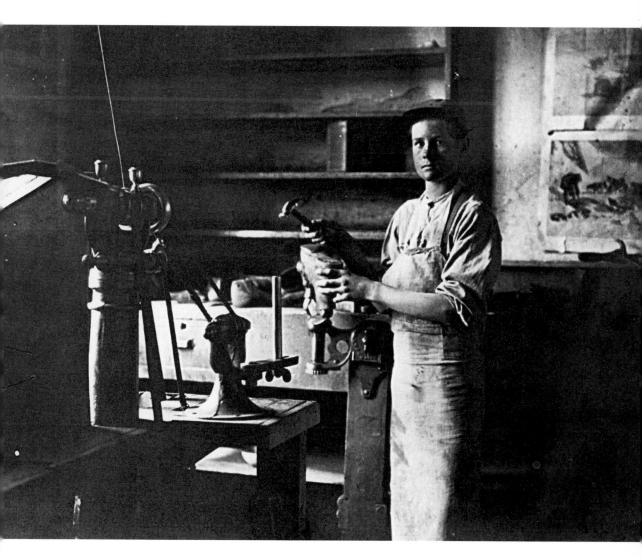

■ TEENAGERS CAUGHT ON THE ROAD BY THE POLICE WERE SOMETIMES SENT TO REFORM SCHOOL TO LEARN A TRADE. *(Courtesy of the Library of Congress)*

They broke the cuffs with a rock and made their way to a jungle, where they were welcomed. Shortly after they settled down, they saw two men approach the camp. At first they seemed like fellow 'boes, but when they came nearer, one of the two drew a gun and ordered everyone to stand still. The detective whom Bill had kicked off the train had tracked them to the jungle. But before Bill and Tully could react, one of the hoboes knocked the gun out of the policeman's hand. Bill jumped up and knocked him unconscious. The remaining hoboes subdued the other policeman, handcuffed them to each other around a tree, and then took off.

Like many road kids, Tully and Bill knew that they were despised and hated by respectable society and that most police officers would arrest or even kill them given the chance. By the end of the nineteenth century, the hobo and the tramp were considered by most of the country a plague on society. There was a great public outcry to get rid of them by any means—and in response, many law enforcement agencies acted with incredible brutality, in complete violation of the law.

5

Terrors and Tragedies of the Road

Early every morning the sheriff comes around
He gives us rotten herring that weighs a quarter pound.
With coffee like tobacco juice and bread that's hard and stale.
And this is the way they fed us boes in Cecil County Jail.

— BILL QUIRKE, HOBO

Most "good citizens" had no interest in the distinctions between tramps and hoboes. As far as they were concerned, anyone without a home and a steady job was a tramp, to be feared and despised by righteous people. One minister expressed the common public attitude when he wrote that the tramp was "a drinker, habit-formed, diseased, filthy, vermin-covered, hungry, helpless, hopeless, hell bound . . . without home, without friends and without God."

Tramps were considered members of a dangerous class. Many "respectable" people felt they were products of laziness and morally depraved. They were accused of committing every crime, from hijacking to robbery to murder. A poem written by John McIntosh in 1877 went:

> *Oh what will be done with the tramp—the scamp*
> *The curse of our Yankee nation*
> *A nuisance is he*
> *And a mystery*
> *Defying interrogation*

As far as the press was concerned, tramps had no rights. One newspaper wrote, "They were at war with social institutions." On July 12, 1877, the *Chicago Tribune* suggested tramps should be eliminated by poisoning them: "The simplest plan is to put a little strychnine or arsenic in the meat and other supplies furnished to the tramp. This produces death in a comparatively short time, is a warning to other tramps to keep out of the neighborhood . . . and saves one's chickens . . . from constant disruption."

In Westchester County, New York, a law was passed (but never enforced) that would require the superintendent of the county poorhouse to flood the building with water to a height of six feet so that "tramps and vagrants can be placed there and then let the water be

■ HOBOES AND TRAMPS WERE CONTINUALLY BEING RAIDED BY THE POLICE. HERE, THEY ARE ROUTED FROM A BARN IN WHICH THEY HAVE BEEN SLEEPING, AND ARRESTED. (*Used by permission of the Antiquarian and Landmark Society, Inc., of Connecticut*)

turned on to bail or be submerged." If the tramp did not bail the water out fast enough, he would drown. *The New York Herald* in 1878 thought there was a better way to rid society of tramps. "The best meal that can be given to tramps is a leaden one and it should be supplied in sufficient quantity to satisfy the most voracious appetite." When one farmer in the Midwest killed two tramps, he was applauded in the local press and other tramps were advised to take warning from his act.

One way communities tried to keep tramps out was to pass stiff vagrancy laws. Thirty days in jail was the norm, but some judges handed down stiffer sentences. When a tramp was sentenced to three years at hard labor in prison for entering a yard without the owner's permission, the appeals-court judge denied a request to overturn the sentence. In his opinion upholding the conviction he wrote:

> The tramp is a public enemy. He is a nomad, a wanderer of the face of the earth with his hand against every honest man, woman and child insofar as they do not promptly and fully supply his demands. He is a thief, a robber, often a murderer and always a nuisance. The objection that this act presumes cruel and unusual punishment we think not well taken. . . . Imprisonment at hard labor is neither cruel or unusual.

Another judge expressed the opinion that "the penitentiary is the only institution which holds any chance of the conversion of the tramp from the error of his ways." In Missouri at the end of the nineteenth century, four hoboes were sold under a law that allowed the state to make legal slaves of them. Two of the men were bought for two dollars and set free. One was bought for seventy-five cents by a farmer, who put him to work. The fourth man was sent back to jail because no one bid for him.

The fact that many of these punishments were unconstitutional was of no concern to many local courts and sheriffs. One writer expressed the common sentiment: "He [the tramp] has no more rights than the sow that wallows in the gutter or the lost dog that hovers in city squares." Tramps and hoboes were always at the mercy of policemen, who could order them around at will. Tom Kromer described a typical encounter. He had not eaten for two days and while passing by a restaurant saw a man inside eating a chicken. As he stopped to watch, he suddenly felt a hand on his shoulder. It was a policeman.

"What the hell are you doing," he said. "I'm just watching a guy eat a chicken. Can't a guy watch another guy eat a chicken?" I replied. "Wise guy. I know what to do with wise guys." The cop slugged me across the face with his hand, hard. I fell back against the building. His hands were on the holsters by his side. What can I do? . . . He will plug me if I do anything.

■ TOWNSPEOPLE OFTEN CHASED HOBOES OUT OF TOWN, BEATING THEM AS THEY TRIED TO FLEE.

In many jails, hoboes and tramps were brutally treated. Often they were charged with crimes someone else had committed. This was how many police departments "solved" cases—they'd accuse an innocent hobo of the crime; the judge would find him guilty; and he would be sentenced. The case would then be closed even though the wrong man was convicted.

In one town in Iowa, hoboes were forced to run a gauntlet of men and women who threw stones at them and beat them with whips as they ran. In Florida, the police set up an electrically wired chair in which hoboes were seated and then given a jolt of electricity. In another town, tramps were chained to trees to let the mosquitoes feed on them, and then turned loose.

The worst place for a hobo to get arrested was in the South—especially for a black man. There were not many black hoboes on the road until the Great Depression of 1929. One study made at the turn of the century estimated that only 8 percent of the hobo/tramp population was black. One reason for the small number of black hoboes was that even though blacks might be accepted by most white hoboes, they would not be allowed to beg or seek work in most white communities. Many who did were jailed, sentenced to long prison terms, beaten, or killed just for being poor, black, and on the road.

The South's hatred of all tramps and hoboes, especially those from the North, made them easy victims for local sheriffs looking for convict labor. They would arrest hoboes and turn them over to judges, who would sentence them to hard labor for six months to a year. After they were convicted, they could be leased out to farmers to harvest crops, or to contractors, who forced them to build roads or work on the brutal turpentine farms. The sheriffs and judges received a fee for each convict they leased out. Other hoboes were sent to the notorious chain gangs, forced to carry an iron ball and chain and wear striped uniforms. Whenever they walked, they had to carry the ball. Thousands of hoboes died from this kind of treatment.

■ HOBOES COULD EXPECT NO MERCY IF THEY WERE SENT TO PRISON. THEY WERE OVER-
WORKED AND OFTEN BEATEN. MANY DIED THERE. (*Courtesy of the Library of Congress*

Yet despite all this hostility and violence, tramps and hoboes kept wandering across America. During a depression, many communities were overwhelmed by their sheer numbers. They crowded the jails and clogged the courts. Often judges had no choice but to let them go. When the railroads complained, the city officials told them that the hoboes were their problem and they should solve it. In reality, the problem was not solvable.

Meanwhile, a few leading people of the day were beginning to see that hoboes were not simply men who were lazy and didn't want to work. Allan Pinkerton, the famous private detective whose agency enforced the railroads' policy against hoboes riding trains,

■ ALLAN PINKERTON, THE PRIVATE DETECTIVE WHO PROTECTED THE RAILROADS FROM HOBOES AND TRAMPS. *(Courtesy of the Pinkerton Agency)*

was keenly aware that most tramps were victims of hard times. In his book *Strikers, Communists, Tramps, and Detectives*, Pinkerton wrote that he saw them as "guerrillas on the outskirts of civilization." He himself had once been a tramp journeyman in Scotland, "carrying the bundle and the stick . . . seeking work and not getting it." He concluded: "What other recourse had these people but to turn tramp and beg and pilfer to sustain life? . . . There is no doubt that a majority of these now on the road are there from necessity and not from choice."

Many leading intellectuals saw the industrial revolution as giving birth to the tramp. Henry George, one of the leading social thinkers of the nineteenth century, wrote in *Progress and Poverty*: "The tramp comes with the locomotive, and almshouses and prisons are surely the marks of 'material progress' as are costly dwellings, rich warehouses and magnificent churches."

Hamlin Garland, who became a famous writer in the late nineteenth century, remembered in *A Son of the Middle Border* his initial anxiety about the hobo farmworkers who helped his father during harvest time:

> Most of the harvest help were nomads who had followed the line of ripening wheat from Missouri northward, and were not the most profitable companion for boys of fifteen. They reached our neighborhood in July, arriving like a flock of alien unclean birds and vanished into the North in September as mysteriously as they had appeared.

Garland's attitude toward hoboes changed when it was his turn to tramp on the road. After being told by one woman from whom he and his brother had begged food, "We don't feed tramps," Garland reflected:

> We came to understand the bitter rebellion of the tramp. I had been brought up to believe that labor was honorable, that idlers were to be despised, but now as I sat with bowed head, cold, hungry and penniless,

knowing that I must go forth at daylight, seeking work, the world seemed a very hostile place to me.

To the tramp who suffered from not being able to find work, it was disheartening to also suffer abuse. One hobo wrote:

> I have crossed 17 states in a year and was offered 6 weeks work. I have faced starvation for month after month. When the thermometer was down 30 below zero last winter I slept on the road. I have been two or three days without food. When, in God's name, I asked for something to keep body and soul together, I have been repulsed as a "tramp" and "vagabond" by those who thank God for His mercy and Praised Charities.

There were some who tried to change the image of the tramp and hobo in the public's mind. At the turn of the century, an organization called the International Brotherhood of Welfare Associates (IBWA) was formed. Its purpose was to promote a positive image of hoboes as well as help educate them.

The IBWA was the dream of one of the most unusual men to become involved with the hobo world. His name was James Eads How, and he came from a wealthy family of St. Louis, Missouri. His grandfather was the mayor of St. Louis before the Civil War, and his father was a chief executive with the Wabash Railroad. How himself was a physician, but never practiced. Instead, he became a champion of the hobo. Refusing the comfort that his family's wealth could have given him, he chose to live in near poverty, renting a small room with little furniture, eating only vegetables, and wearing old clothes. How had inherited about half a million dollars—worth about $6 million in today's money. Most of it he spent on the IBWA or gave to the poor.

In 1912 How organized a series of hobo colleges in many major cities. He believed that hoboes were intelligent and knew from personal experience many economic and social realities that the outstanding thinkers of the time were writing about. Many people ridiculed

How for his university for bums. But one woman hobo, Boxcar Bertha, angrily defended the idea when she wrote: "Hoboes are not a bunch of dumb ignoramuses. They have an interest in and a capacity for good lectures and intellectual food."

The colleges were not formal institutions of learning but lecture halls in which famous thinkers discussed issues like socialism, industrial law, political science, and economics. Hoboes debated issues with the speakers and with each other.

How also published a newspaper for hoboes called the *Hobo News*. Later others took the same name for their papers. How's paper contained many articles on social and political issues, but it also carried a number of puns and jokes. Later editions of the paper would carry far more jokes than serious articles.

Another man who helped promote the hobo cause was Jeff Davis, who was himself a hobo. Davis organized a group called the Hoboes of America. He called himself the King of the Hoboes and defended his title against many challengers. More practical-minded than How, Davis tried to set up a series of what he called Hotel de Ginks, which were residences where hoboes could eat and sleep and get a shave and a bath when times were tough.

The hotels quickly failed, but Davis continued his crusade. He tried to get employment for hoboes so that they wouldn't have to rely on the slave markets. He also fought against legal injustice and against vagrancy laws. For all his self-promotion, he worked hard to bring about reforms that would benefit the hobo.

Another supporter of the hobo was Rich Eddie Brown, a man many considered eccentric. Rich Eddie had sufficient money to live a normal life. He liked to dine in New York's best restaurants; then, after dinner, he would change his evening clothes for those of a tramp, and panhandle on the street. Rich Eddie would often flip a freight to the Midwest, where he worked in the berry fields. He preached the virtues of the hobo to anyone who would listen: "I have seen men huddled before offices in the bitterest of weather, their pockets and stomachs empty, few of them half-sufficiently clad, but all of them eager to take on any kind of work, no matter how heavy it might be or what the wages."

Rich Eddie's description of the hobo's desperate search for a job was an accurate one. But even the hobo's traditional patience and acceptance of hard times was coming to an end. Working conditions continued to get worse. There was a general feeling among migrant workers that something needed to be done. Early in the twentieth century, a militant labor organization appeared that not only agreed with the necessity of change but was willing to do something about it. It defined the relationship between workers and owners as a state of war and offered to lead the hobo into battle for better working conditions and wages. The era of the Wobblies had been born.

■ MANY HARVEST WORKERS WERE HOBOES. THE I.W.W. WAS EXTREMELY SUCCESSFUL IN ORGANIZING THEM INTO THE UNION IN CERTAIN AREAS OF THE COUNTRY. (*Courtesy of the Library of Congress*)

6

The Wobblies

It is we who plowed the prairies; built the cities where they trade;
Dug the mines and built the workshops; endless miles of railroad laid.
Now we stand, outcast and starving, mid the wonders we have made.
But the Union makes us strong.

— RALPH CHAPLIN, "SOLIDARITY FOREVER"

In 1910, out of approximately 10 million unskilled workers in America, some 3 million were migratory hoboes. They lived a life of constant insecurity, never knowing where their next job would be or where their next meal was coming from.

Most hoboes traveled in the West. In the East, industries required stable labor, and often whole families worked in a factory. In the West, the three major industries—lumber, construction, and agriculture—required seasonal labor. This created a vast army of unskilled or semiskilled hoboes who were constantly floating from job to job, living in the worst conditions, working for the lowest wages, and lacking hope for the future.

Hoboes were always exploited. California landowners held thousands of acres of rich farmland, and welcomed hoboes in order to make sure that they had a large supply of cheap labor for their farms. Hoboes would line up in front of a bank in Bakersfield, California, to receive a quarter from Henry Miller, the largest landholder in the state. He would also send some out to his ranches, instructing his foremen to: "Never refuse a tramp a meal, but never give him more than one meal. A tramp should be a tramp and keep on tramping. Never let the tramps

INTERNATION**L'ABOR AGE**
355

IF YOU DON'T SEE THE JOB
YOU WANT COME IN & INQUIRE
IT COST NOTHING

WE·SHIP·FOR·THE·ERIE·RR
TRACK·WORK·AND·FREIGHT·HANDLING
$2.20 PER ½ DAY·BONUS·$2.50·PER·MO. BUFFALO·DIVISION 2.40 PER DAY
BINGHAMPTON   ELMIRA   CORNING
SPRING·VALLEY   355   NANUET
SPARKILL·PATERSON   HOWELL

CONSTRUCTION
NOW·PAYING $3.00 GOOD
NO·MONEY REQUIRED BOARD
8 CENTS·FARE

COAL·MINE   IRON·MINE
W.·VIRGI   N.
86 TO 1 $3
PER G.

NOW $3.00

EVER
8.00
2.75

■ SOME UNEMPLOYMENT AGENCIES ADVERTISED JOBS FOR HOBOES FOR A FEE. MANY OF THEM WERE CALLED "SLAVE MARKETS" BECAUSE THEY CHEATED HOBOES BY CHARGING THEM FEES FOR JOBS THAT WOULD UNDERPAY OR DID NOT EXIST. *(Used by permission of the George Eastman House)*

eat with the other men. Make them wait until the men are through and then let them eat off the same plates." As a result, the route to Henry Miller's camp became known as "the Dirty Plate Route." One man who worked for Miller described at a congressional hearing in 1916 the way hoboes were treated at his farms:

> There was almost always a shortage of sleeping quarters and those were often lousy and foul. Bathing facilities were unknown and washing facilities inadequate. Often men slept on manure piles to keep warm during the frosty nights with only . . . boxes or sugar barrels to separate the sleeper from the steaming, stinking refuse.

One way hoboes tried to find guaranteed work was through the "slave markets." The slave markets advertised jobs, hired men, and provided transportation to the work site, for a fee. This was usually one or two dollars, or more if the markets would bear. Hoboes were easy victims for the many "sharks" (dishonest operators of slave markets). A hobo paid a fee to a shark, usually on the promise that the job he was getting paid high wages and provided decent room and board, plus return transportation when the job was finished. But when the hobo arrived at the work site, he might find only 400 jobs available—and 5,000 other men, who had also paid a fee. Many times the wages paid were lower than had been promised, and the hobo had to either take what was offered or leave. If a man refused to take a job or was turned down, he would have to use his own resources to get out of town. Nor was there any chance of getting his dollar back from the slave market that sent him there in the first place. The slave-market owner would pocket the extra money, even though he knew that there were not enough jobs available for all the men he had sent. He knew it was standard practice for companies to ask for more workers than they needed. In this way, they could keep wages low and make sure they had a wide selection of men to choose from.

Another racket colluded in by the slave markets and employers was for foremen to fire laborers, or work them so hard they would quit after a few weeks. In this way, new men would have to be sent to the job, generating new fees for the slave market. Many slave-market operators could make thousands of extra dollars on a job by sending a new group of men every two to three weeks. Usually, they would bribe the foreman to make sure workers didn't last longer than their first paychecks.

Even when the jobs were legitimate, the working conditions were often unbearable. Some men worked twelve hours a day, seven days a week for $1.50 to $2.00 a day, out of which they had to pay for their own food and board. The food was often disgusting. Meat and fish were rancid and sometimes crawling with maggots. In some places, work crews had to buy food from a store owned by the company. The prices were far higher than at other stores. Red Doran, a hobo organizer, testified before Congress about the general working conditions of lumberjacks: "Camps were unsanitary, abominable places. . . . Many times there was not any hay, let alone mattresses. The grub was mighty poor. . . . Sanitary conditions poor, little or no provision made for bathing, and dirty, filthy animal life was in abundance."

As a result of these labor practices, many hoboes were on the road a good part of the year, traveling thousands of miles for work and laboring at a variety of jobs. They might work as roughnecks in the oil fields of Texas, timberbeasts in the logging camps of Washington, shovel stiffs on a railroad in Utah, harvester stiffs in Kansas and Nebraska. In between these jobs, they might earn a little money chopping wood, cleaning windows, fixing chimneys, cutting grass, shoveling snow, and doing hundreds of other handyman jobs. One job itinerary, of a hobo named Fred, went as follows:

JOB	STATE	HOURS (per day)	WAGES (per day)	TIME
Building logging cars	N.Y.	12	1.62	7 months
Deckhand	N.Y.	12	1.00	4 weeks
Loading supplies	Ohio	15	2.00	2 weeks
Construction	Wisc.	10	1.55	2 weeks

Land worker	Mont.	8	2.85	5 weeks
Farm labor	Minn.	12	.50	1 day
Longshoreman	Ill.	10	2.16	5 days

Fred worked an average of eleven hours a day. Only one job offered an eight-hour day, and that was for the federal government in Montana. Without it Fred's average working day would have been almost twelve hours long. At least three of the jobs required seven days of work a week. To work at these seven jobs, Fred had to travel almost 2,000 miles. He needed an average of three weeks to find a new job. The main reason he left most of the jobs was because the work was too hard. The jobs he wanted to keep were short-term.

To get work, Fred had to pay at least one day's salary to the slave market. He was fortunate in that the jobs were real and he was hired. In addition, he usually had to pay for his room and board, which cost an average of $4.50 a week. He also had to flip freights to get to the jobs. On the way, he would seldom have problems with train crews, because employers had successfully pressured the railroad to let hoboes ride without interference as long as they were providing needed labor. However, after a job was finished, the brakemen tried to extort money from Fred and others for allowing them to ride. When Fred refused to pay, he was ditched.

Fred's life was no different from that of tens of thousands of other working stiffs. They all hated the conditions under which they were forced to work, yet they saw no way out unless conditions changed. There were labor unions, but none for hoboes. Yet hoboes were keenly aware that all around them a great industrial war had been taking place since the Civil War between the owners of the factories, railroads, and mines of America and their workers. Thousands of hoboes were, in fact, victims of these struggles, having been fired when they dared to strike or ask for better working conditions. Since no other company in the area would hire a striker, many took to the road to find a job.

In addition, a number of socialists, anarchists, and other radicals traveled across the country organizing strikes, speaking and agitating. Some of them passed through hobo jungles, spreading their ideas about socialism and communism to the men gathered there. A number of these agitators were women. Because so much was happening so fast and they needed to move around the country quickly, they didn't have time to ride slow-moving freights. Instead, they decked Pullman cars on fast passenger trains that carried them hundreds and sometimes thousands of miles across country. They flattened themselves on their stomachs, hands over the car's sides, with their legs pressed against ventilation shutters to keep from falling off. It was a dangerous and daring way to ride, and there were very few men who would have had the nerve to do what these socialist women did.

Out of this labor turmoil the I.W.W.—the Industrial Workers of the World—was born in 1905, when some of the best-known leaders of American radical movements gathered at a convention in Chicago. The meeting was chaired by "Big Bill" Haywood, the fiery and dynamic secretary of the Western Federation of Miners. On the platform with him were the legendary labor organizer Mother Jones, who had been organizing miners for forty years; Eugene Debs, the socialist candidate for President of the United States and former head of the American Railroad Union; and Lucy Parsons, the widow of anarchist Albert Parsons who was framed and executed for planting a bomb that killed eight policemen. Their joint efforts resulted in the formation of a union that would incorporate all workers in America, regardless of their job, race, or religion, into One Big Union—the Industrial Workers of the World. It was the purpose of the I.W.W. to lead the workers to victory over the owners who oppressed them.

The basic political philosophy of the I.W.W. was that a class war existed between the workers and their bosses. The preamble to the union's constitution stated: "Between these two classes, a struggle must go on until the workers of the world organize as a class, take possession

■ "BIG BILL" HAYWOOD WAS ONE OF THE LEADING ORGANIZERS OF THE I.W.W. EVENTUALLY HE FLED THE UNITED STATES TO AVOID BEING IMPRISONED ON FALSE CHARGES. *(Courtesy of the Library of Congress)*

of the earth and the machinery of production, and abolish the wage system." The I.W.W. promoted itself as a union ready to use violence whenever necessary to secure the rights of workers. Actually, the threat of violence was more talk than action. Most of the members were far more conservative than some of their leaders, and many hoboes were unsympathetic to violence.

Shortly after its formation, the I.W.W. was given the nickname "Wobblies." Although nobody really knows how the name originated, one legend is that a Chinese cook who fed I.W.W. members for free could not correctly pronounce the name of their union. He was supposed to have called it "I-Wobble-Wobble." The name Wobblies stuck.

Big Bill Haywood saw the potential for recruitment among the hobo and migrant population when he stated: "We are going down into the gutter to get the mass of workers and bring them up to a decent place of living." The I.W.W. went after the "wage slaves" and shovel stiffs. There was some debate about whether workers who were constantly on the move could be organized. The union leaders decided that if the workers could not come to the union, the union would go to the workers. Organizers like Joe Walsh and his wife began to spread the I.W.W. gospel to lumberjacks, miners, railroad workers, and harvesters, giving them I.W.W. buttons to wear and I.W.W. books to read. By 1910, the I.W.W. had launched a full campaign to recruit the wandering worker. Articles in the I.W.W. newspaper *The Industrial Worker* were written to attract members. One editorial said: "A Hobo and a Tramp are nice names to have the boss call you after he has worked the hell out of you and taken the greater share of the production of your toil. It's up to you. One union for all is the only cure."

The Wobbly organizers were described by one observer as "lonely hobo workers, usually malnourished and in need of medical care." Their minds were "stamped by the lowest, most miserable labor conditions and outlook which American industrialism produces." The organizers first went into the jungles and rode the trains to recruit members. They drove out the criminal tramp elements, cleaned up the camps, and pressured men to join. They sometimes threatened them with pick handles; men who refused to join and carry the red union card might be thrown off trains. A man who refused to carry one was considered a "scissorbill," or strikebreaker. Some hoboes complained of the rough treatment but most joined willingly, aware that the Wobblies were fighting for them.

One of the most effective Wobbly recruiting techniques was singing radical labor songs. The I.W.W. was fortunate to have several talented folksong writers. The best-known were Joe Hill, who wrote "The Preacher and the Slave"; T-Bone Slim; and Ralph Chaplin. They wrote songs about the struggles and sufferings of the workingman, which were gathered together in *The Little Red Song Book.* The composers used the melodies of popular songs of the day, but changed the romantic or religious lyrics into ones that reflected the struggles and eventual victory of the workers:

> *They have bullied and oppressed us, but still our union grows*
> *But we're going to find a way boys, shorter hours and better pay boys.*
> *And we're going to win the day boys where the Fraser River flows.*

The Wobblies attracted audiences with their songs, their fiery rhetoric, and their street theater. In one "play" they performed, a well-dressed man staggered out of an alley in a poor section of town, crying that he had been robbed. When people gathered around him, not realizing he was acting, and asked who robbed him, he would suddenly cry out, "I've been robbed by the capitalist bloodsuckers." Then the organizers would make their pitch to the crowd. They would pass out literature and recruit new members into the One Big Union. They were surprised to find that *The Little Red Song Book* was always the most popular item. "It sold like hotcakes," Walsh reported. Soon hoboes all over the West were singing songs without the book. Their favorite was "Hallelujah, I'm a Bum":

Oh why don't you work
Like other men do.
How the hell can I work
When there's no work to do?

Hallelujah, I'm a bum.
Hallelujah, bum again
Hallelujah, give us a handout
To revive us again.

One location where Wobbly organizers gathered to speak was in front of the slave markets in the cities. No institution exploited hoboes more and no institution was more hated by them. The fiery tone of the speeches soon alarmed city leaders, who began to ban the Wobblies from speaking. This led to the famous free speech struggles, which lasted from 1910 to 1916. Large groups of Wobblies would ride freight cars into a town that had banned their rallies. They were usually arrested and imprisoned until the jails were overcrowded. In 1910, Frank Little, a Wobbly organizer who was part Indian, organized a free speech movement in Fresno, California. He targeted his activities against the low wages some of the contractors were paying. The contractors called in the police, who immediately imprisoned Little. He sent a call for help and hundreds of men jumped on freights and headed for Fresno. When the police started to stop trains, the Wobblies walked the 244 miles instead, crossing the Siskiyou Mountains, which were then covered with three feet of snow. Many of the men were poorly dressed and lacked adequate shoes, but they made the trip.

Once inside the jails, the Wobblies tormented their guards with lectures on the class war and songs. They also demonstrated inside the prison. Fire hoses were turned on them, but they refused to quit. Finally, the mayor of Fresno, feeling that the battle was about to escalate out of control, began to release small groups of prisoners. He also rescinded the ban on free speech.

■ DURING THE FREE SPEECH CAMPAIGN IN SEATTLE, WASHINGTON, MOBS WOULD AT-
TACK WOBBLIES AND BURN THEIR PROPERTY. (*Courtesy of the Library of Congress*)

The Wobblies tried the same tactic in San Diego, but here they met fierce resistance. The city officials met the free speech demonstrations with hoses and arrests, and the newspapers cried for the blood of Wobblies. The *Los Angeles Times* editorialized: "Hanging is none too good for them. They would be much better dead, for they are absolutely useless in the human economy; they are the waste material of creation and should be drained off into the sewer of oblivion, there to rot in cold obstruction like any other excrement."

The situation was made worse when an employee of the *Times*, a newspaper totally opposed to labor unions, planted a bomb that killed twenty-one people when it exploded. The bomb had been intended only to destroy property. Two men who pleaded guilty were sent to prison. But even though the bombers were not Wobblies, the union's enemies quickly linked the tragedy with the I.W.W. They formed vigilante committees in San Diego that captured demonstrators before they could disembark from the train, viciously beat them, and drove them out of the county. Albert Tucker, who was one of the Wobblies captured, described what happened in a report:

> They closed in around the flat car on which we were on and began clubbing and knocking and pulling men off by their heels, so inside a half hour they had pulled us all off the train and then bruised and bleeding we were lined up. They marched us around several times and then picking out a man they thought was a leader and giving him an extra beating. In the morning . . . they marched us out to the county line, forced us to kiss the flag and run a gauntlet of 106 men, everyone striking as hard as they could with pick-ax handles. They broke one man's legs and everyone was beaten black and blue and was bleeding from a dozen wounds.

The free speech movement reached its height of violence in Everett, Washington, in 1916. After a group of I.W.W. organizers had been viciously beaten and run out of town, the Wobblies decided to defy the free speech ban. They organized two ferryboats filled with men to sail to Everett and carry out a free speech crusade. When the first boat tried

to land, the passengers were greeted by gunfire from a vigilante com-
mittee led by a local sheriff. At least five Wobblies and two vigilantes
died. Seventy-four Wobblies were indicted and tried for the deaths of
the vigilantes. But the jury believed that the vigilantes were acciden-
tally killed by members of their own group. When they acquitted the
first defendant, the rest were set free.

While the free speech struggle gave the Wobblies a great deal of
publicity, their main goal was to win better conditions for workers.
The I.W.W. had won several major strikes in New England and New
Jersey, but the critical battlefield was in the West. In 1913, they led a
strike at the Durst Ranch, where thousands of migrants worked in the
fields without water and where there were only six toilets for over 2,800
workers. Men, women, and children started work at four o'clock in the
morning and picked fruits and vegetables through the heat of the day—
which at times reached over 100 degrees. As the organizers called a
strike, the local sheriff arrived with his deputies. A confrontation took
place and four men, two on each side, were killed. Hundreds of Wobblies were arrested and some were sentenced to life in prison. As a
result of the incident, the State of California investigated the working
conditions at the Durst Ranch and did legislate some reforms.

Overall, the Wobblies lost more strikes than they won. But the fact
that they persisted in face of tremendous hostility against them and
that they did sometimes win against terrible odds converted many hoboes to their cause.

Every Wobbly organizer knew that his life was on the line. In 1915,
Joe Hill, a folksinger who wandered throughout the West, organizing
strikes and writing songs about the struggles, was charged with killing
a grocer and his son in Salt Lake City, Utah. Although there was no
direct evidence to link him to the crime, Hill was sentenced to death
and executed despite the fact that people from all over America and
the rest of the world asked the governor of Utah to commute his sentence to life in prison. The governor refused and Joe Hill was killed.

His last words were "Don't mourn, boys: Organize!" He became a legend and the folk song "I Dreamed I Saw Joe Hill Last Night" was written about him. In the song, the ghost of Joe Hill says that he still lives wherever people are struggling for their rights.

■ CONDITIONS IN THE LOGGING CAMPS WERE BRUTAL. I.W.W. ORGANIZERS WHO TRIED TO BRING LOGGERS INTO THE UNION WERE OFTEN BEATEN AND MURDERED. (*Courtesy of the Library of Congress*)

Another Wobbly martyr was Frank Little, one of the best I.W.W. organizers. He was feared and hated by companies throughout the West. He was organizing a strike in Butte, Montana, when six masked men, believed to be company guards, broke into his room one night, took him outside, and lynched him. In Centralia, Washington, in 1919, the owners of the local lumber companies recruited the American Legion to drive the Wobblies out of town. During an Armistice Day parade, the Legion charged the I.W.W. headquarters. Three legionnaires were killed in the rush. Wesley Everett, a lumberjack who had served in France during World War I, fought back. Everett was in uniform when the mob went after him. He killed another legionnaire before he was captured. That night he was taken out of his jail cell and lynched; his body was mutilated. A thousand other Wobblies were arrested, and seven were convicted of second-degree murder and sentenced to life in prison.

The I.W.W. managed to survive the many attempts of local and state governments to destroy it. But it could not withstand the power of the federal government. In 1916, when America entered World War I, it became a crime to interfere with the war effort. Union leaders knew that the federal government would try to destroy it if given the chance. As a result, it carefully avoided making any antiwar statements. This made no difference. Opponents of the union charged that it was antiwar and pro-German. There was no evidence to support this, although some I.W.W. members who were bitterly opposed to the war did speak out as individuals. This gave the U.S. Justice Department the excuse it was looking for. In 1918, it launched a series of raids on the Wobblies. Hundreds of men were arrested and put on trial for being disloyal to the government and interfering with the war. The leadership was given extremely long terms in prison, from twenty to thirty years. The Wobbly newspaper was banned. Bill Haywood fled to the Soviet Union rather than go to jail. (He spent his last days there alone, drinking himself to death.) The other leaders were all pardoned after a

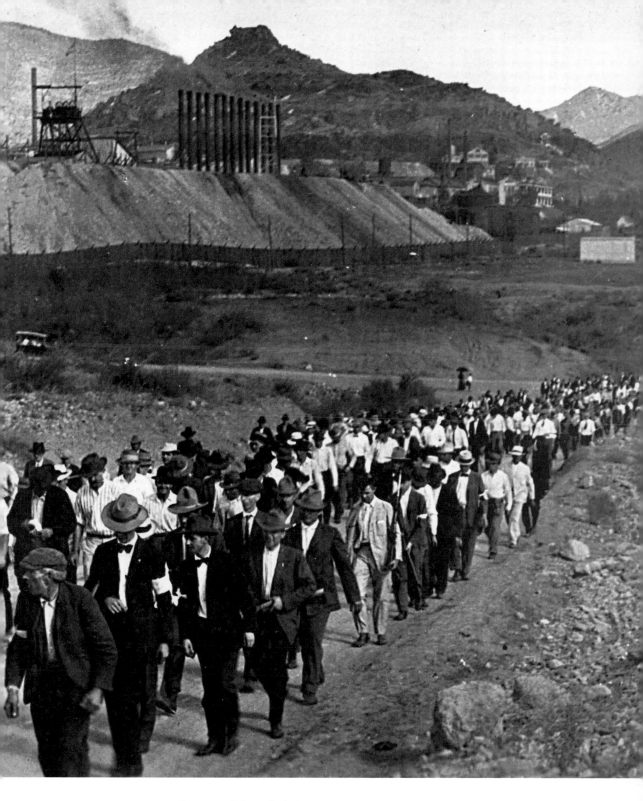

■ WITH THE END OF WORLD WAR I, WOBBLIES WERE ROUNDED UP BY THE FEDERAL GOVERNMENT AND IMPRISONED OR DEPORTED FOR THEIR IDEAS AND BELIEFS. (*Courtesy of the Library of Congress*)

few years in prison, but the raids had had their effect: The I.W.W. had been effectively crushed. And while its songs and some of its traditions continued, it was no longer the force for hobo rights it had been during its heyday.

Even though the I.W.W. did not live up to its goal of creating One Big Union, it had planted seeds that bore fruit in the 1930s. Then, once again, the workers rose up—and this time they successfully created the C.I.O., the One Big Union that finally won them the basic right to organize and earn a decent wage. To some degree the Wobbly dream for the workingman had been fulfilled:

> *We had been naught, we shall be all.*
> *The Union makes us free.*

7

Chicago: Hobo Capital of the World

I stood on the corner and almost bust my head
I couldn't earn enough money to buy me a loaf of bread
The tough luck has struck me and the rats is sleeping in my hat

— BLIND LEMON JEFFERSON

Hoboes and tramps suffered many hardships but none was more fierce and relentless than winter. Few could survive on the road during cold weather. Because there was little work and no place to stay, hoboes had to seek shelter until the spring. Some managed to build shacks and huts by the wayside. Others found sympathetic sheriffs who were willing to house them in jail over the winter. (Sheriffs usually received a dollar a day from the town for their care and feeding.) A few risked jail and the chain gang by traveling to the South. But most men on the road headed toward the large cities. Of all the cities in the United States, Chicago held the most attraction. It was the unofficial capital of the hobo world.

Hoboes came to Chicago from all over the United States. The city was the railroad gateway between the east and west coasts. Every day freight trains arrived from every part of the country, carrying their cargo of men. In the course of a winter, an estimated 300,000 to 500,000 hoboes and tramps came to Chicago.

The central area where they congregated was West Madison Street. Once wealthy, this area had been destroyed by the Chicago fire of

■ Chicago was considered the hobo capital of the United States and West Madison Street the center of hobo activities. (*Used by permission of the Chicago Historical Society*)

1871, and West Madison Street gradually became the most notorious district in Chicago. Vice was everywhere. The streets were filled with houses of prostitution, saloons, pawnshops, opium dens, burlesque houses, and pornographic bookstores. Day and night, the area was packed with hoboes, bums and tramps, thieves and dope fiends, pimps and prostitutes, revolutionaries and anarchists, writers and journalists, tourists and students, missionaries and social workers.

West Madison Street was also the home of the bum. Unlike the hobo, who traveled and worked, and the tramp, who just traveled, the bum neither traveled nor worked. The bum was at the end of the line, done in by alcohol. At one time, most bums had been hoboes or tramps but their working and traveling days were over. They settled down in the skid row sections of cities and tried to mooch enough money for the next drink.

Where tramps and hoboes tried to keep their self-respect, bums completely let themselves go. They often dressed in rags and wore mismatched shoes without socks. They slept on the floor of saloons when they were allowed. From morning to night, they were consumed by their search for money for alcohol. One bum described how his day began:

> I got up at 5:30 [A.M.]. Tried to buy 5 cents worth of denat [denatured alcohol used for paint thinner]. They wouldn't sell me 5 cents worth. I bummed a dime and bought 15 cents worth of denatured alcohol from the paint store. Got some water and mixed my drink. My intent was to take one good drink and sober up. But as soon as I had my drink, I forgot all about my intentions and drank all of it.

Food and shelter were also cheap on West Madison Street. If a man had enough money to stake him through the winter, he could eat in restaurants that charged anywhere from three cents to a quarter for a meal, and live in a flophouse where he could sleep on the floor or on a shelf for a nickel a night. For a dime he could get a 5½-foot by 6½-foot space with a mattress and a blanket. And a quarter would get him his own room with a bath on the same floor.

■ WHEN A HOBO RAN OUT OF MONEY, THE ONLY PLACE FOR HIM TO SLEEP WAS ON THE STREETS OR IN SHELTERS. *(Used by permission of the Chicago Historical Society)*

Those who did not have the means to rent a room turned to Chicago's municipal center, where hundreds of men slept in one large room. Before going to sleep, men who knew the ways of public shelters took their shoes off and tied them around their necks, and put their clothes under their pillows. An expert thief could steal the shoes and even the pants off a sleeping man. For many men it was difficult to fall asleep. All night they were kept awake by others who coughed, spat, snored, moaned, and had hallucinations. At seven A.M., everyone had to be out of bed, even if he was sick.

The center provided edible food. In the morning, toast, coffee, and rolled oats were served. Lunch was often a bologna sandwich and coffee. A vegetable stew or pea soup, beets, and coffee were served for

■ MANY HOBOES SLEPT IN CHEAP FLOPHOUSES WHERE THE FLOOR COST A NICKEL AND A BED A DIME PER NIGHT. (*Used by permission of the Antiquarian and Landmark Society, Inc., of Connecticut*)

■ IN THE WINTERTIME,
MANY HOBOES AND
TRAMPS HUNG OUT IN
SALOONS, WHERE
DRINKS WERE CHEAP
AND FOOD WAS FREE.
(*Used by permission of
the Antiquarian and
Landmark Society, Inc.,
of Connecticut*)

dinner. A man might have to wait on line for up to two hours for a meal. To avoid this, some men, after finishing a meal, lined up immediately for the next one. They often spread newspapers on the floor at the head of the line and went to sleep until it was time to eat again.

There were many other places that a wanderer could find help. The missions were one possibility, but a price had to be paid for assistance: two to three hours of religious services. Many men faked being saved in order to get coffee and doughnuts sooner. Missionaries referred to them as "doughnut Christians." Some men, however, enjoyed singing the hymns.

If a hobo had a little money, there were three places he would visit—a burlesque house, a house of prostitution, and a saloon. The first two visits usually lasted a limited time. The third could last all day. Until Prohibition became the law in 1919, a saloon was a place where a man could get a large glass of beer for a nickel. Lunch was free.

The most famous saloon in Chicago during the late nineteenth and early twentieth century was the Workingman's Exchange. It was owned by another legendary Chicago figure—Michael "Hinky Dink" Kenna, a corrupt but colorful and very powerful politician in Chicago. The bar of the Workingman's Exchange was a hundred feet long. The saloon was nationally known as a place where a hobo or tramp could get a drink, a free lunch, and help. It had three rules: no orchestra, no women, and no selling to minors. Hoboes and tramps would stream in all day long. They were made welcome because almost all of them would sell their votes for a few drinks. At every election Hinky Dink rounded up vagrants and paid each man cash or liquor to vote four or five times for his candidate, using a different name each time. The famous English writer H. G. Wells visited the saloon and remarked:

> He [Alderman Kenna] is very kind to all his crowd. He helps them when they are in trouble, even if it is trouble with the police; he helps them

find employment when they are down on their luck. . . . He tells them how to vote, a duty they might neglect, and sees that they do it properly.

But the most famous, and most theatrical, figure in the West Madison community was Dr. Ben Reitman, who was one of the best friends Chicago's hoboes and tramps ever had. Reitman was a striking-looking figure with a gray suit, long, flowing hair down his back, and a Buffalo Bill mustache. When Reitman was a child, he and his mother and brother were abandoned by his father. Ben helped to support his family by working on the streets, selling newspapers, shining shoes, stealing coal from the railroad yards, running errands for prostitutes and pimps,

■ BEN REITMAN CALLED HIMSELF KING OF THE HOBOES AND WORKED ALL HIS LIFE FOR THEIR BETTERMENT. (*Used by permission of the Chicago Historical Society*)

and bumming free meals in saloons. At the age of twelve, he met two tramps named Ohio Skip and Cincinnati Slim. The next day he was in Ohio. Ben had flipped his first train. The street kid had become a road kid.

Unlike some road kids, Ben returned home periodically. He was extremely bright and went to work in a medical laboratory. The doctors he worked for encouraged him to study medicine, and indeed he earned a medical degree. But for years he refused to give up the road. Even after he had set up a medical practice, the urge to wander constantly overtook him. On impulse, Ben would leave his office to flip a freight. He traveled throughout the United States and Europe and was arrested more than forty times. He often lectured judges on the injustice of vagrancy laws.

Reitman was soon caught up in the social and political currents of the early twentieth century. He joined the Wobblies and took part in the free-speech fights in San Diego, where he was run out of town by local vigilantes who stripped him naked, burned the initials "IWW" into his flesh, and then tarred him and covered him with sagebrush. Neither physical brutality nor imprisonment silenced him. Reitman spoke out for many progressive causes. He was arrested in New York for passing out information on birth control, which was then against the law. He also carried on a passionate love affair with Emma Goldman, who was the leading anarchist of her day. But his true passion was the hobo cause. He once said: "I saw myself as the greatest of the hoboes. The hobo who would save all of them from homeless, womanless, jobless lives."

Reitman staged a number of events that called attention to the condition of the hobo. In 1907 he held a famous banquet for hoboes, to which the press was invited. It was his intention to make the public aware of the plight of the hobo. The guests told stories of their hard life on the road, the many injustices they had suffered, and their desire to find work. Their bitter and grim stories were interrupted from time

■ CALLED THE QUEEN OF ANARCHISTS, EMMA GOLDMAN WAS ONE OF THE LEADING RADICALS IN AMERICA DURING THE EARLY TWENTIETH CENTURY AND WAS AT ONE TIME ROMANTICALLY INVOLVED WITH BEN REITMAN. *(Courtesy of the Library of Congress)*

to time with humor, poetry, and songs. But the press ignored the serious aspect of the dinner, instead making fun of the affair. Still, the banquet established Reitman as a major spokesperson for the hobo.

In 1927, Ben had the opportunity to run a hotel for hoboes. Four gangsters, known as the Four Horsemen—Mike Hoffman, Sol Stearns, Abe Kress, and Phil Denman—owned the infamous Granville Hotel, known for its high-priced prostitutes. A reform mayor had been elected, and he had the hotel constantly raided by the police. Ben was the house doctor for the women who worked there. The owners were debating whether to close it because of police pressure when Hoffman, on an impulse, decided to give the hotel to Reitman for his hoboes and tramps. The Four Horsemen also offered to pay for the bellhops and food. Ben named the hotel God's Kingdom for Hoboes and advertised free food and lodging. The first night over 100 hoboes showed up and drew lots for the 75 rooms. The best room in the hotel went to Dan Spears, an old hobo who had not slept on a bed for years. Rather than dirty the sheets, Spears slept on the floor.

For almost three weeks, the hotel was a paradise not only for hoboes but for many prostitutes and pimps, who came there to help the homeless men. They cooked the food, cleaned the rooms, and joined in the debates and concerts held there. The hotel provided desperately needed shelter during the harsh winter, when many of the traditional lodgings for the homeless were already full. But the hotel was located in a middle-class black neighborhood whose residents objected to hundreds of hoboes wandering about every day. They protested to the city, and after a month the hotel was closed. The hoboes, once again homeless, returned to the flophouses and back alleys for the winter.

The most outstanding achievement in Ben Reitman's crusade was the creation of the Hobo College in Chicago. Ben's involvement was triggered by his encounter with James Eads How, the millionaire who was setting up hobo colleges throughout America. Despite his tendency to publicize everything in a theatrical way, Ben was deadly serious about the college. He saw it as "a service station, clearing house and educational institution for homeless men." Reitman wanted the college to be a place where all kinds of hoboes—workers and tramps— could study everything from politics to law, literature to philosophy, public speaking to English composition. He worked day and night to make his dream a success. He badgered people for money, free tickets to concerts and shows, free clothing, free food, and jobs. He took up collections among the hoboes and tramps who attended, reminding them that they were the ones who benefited most from their contributions. They grumbled and cursed him but came up with money when it was asked for.

The Hobo College was not a university in the usual sense of the word. Reitman had originally hoped to offer two weeks of courses with free room and board for every man who wanted to attend. Instead, the college was open through the winter (the rest of the year most hoboes were on the road looking for work) and consisted of a series of lectures,

■ HOBO COLLEGES WERE FOUNDED IN EVERY MAJOR CITY IN THE UNITED STATES. THEY OFFERED COURSES AND LECTURES ON A VARIETY OF SUBJECTS, AS WELL AS PLAYS AND POETRY READINGS. *(Used by permission of the Chicago Historical Society)*

debates, and concerts. In the one lecture room, which could seat 100 people, the class sat on uncomfortable backless wooden benches that were referred to as "anti-snooze, anti-booze church pews."

The faculty was a mixture of some of the best professors in Chicago, and extraordinary hobo teachers. Not only did outstanding scholars lecture there about psychology, medicine, sociology, law, and economics, but famous hoboes and criminals also spoke. The famous confidence man Yellow Kid Well, who had cheated people of millions of dollars, spoke about finance. Experienced hoboes and tramps talked about subjects such as friendly and hostile towns in America, the art of writing your moniker on a water tank, and the true facts and figures of hobo life.

In 1923, a famous debate was held at the college between the debating team of the University of Chicago and the Hobo College team of Boxcar Bennie, Larry the Loud, and Fred Fourdice. The subject was about the value of a college education. The students were in favor, the hoboes opposed. The hobo team massacred the opposition. It was no surprise. When students at the Hobo College agreed to take an intelligence test, it was discovered that over eighty of them had higher I.Q.'s than the average college senior. There were other debates, not all of which the Hobo College teams won. But they always gave good arguments and were a major attraction not only for their intelligence but their wit and humor as well.

At the end of a term, diplomas were awarded to those who faithfully attended. They read in part:

BE IT KNOWN TO ALL THE WORLD THAT _____ has been a student at the HOBO College and has attended lectures, discussions, clinics, musicals, readings and visits to the art galleries and theaters.

He has also expressed a desire to get an education, better his own condition and build a world that will be without unemployment, poverty, wards, prostitution, ignorance and injustice.

The Hobo College was one part of a world known as hobohemia—a mixture of hobo and intellectual culture. The other two parts were "Bughouse Square" and the Dil Pickle Club. (It was actually the Dill Pickle Club but because the owner was concerned that the name might have been copyrighted, he deliberately misspelled Dill.)

Bughouse Square was a part of Chicago's Washington Park where speakers stood on soapboxes and freely advocated any idea they liked. In his unpublished autobiography, Slim Brundage described the scene as follows:

> By three o'clock in the afternoon, there must have been two thousand people there. Here the speakers were completely ringed by people. Usually the best speakers would be on the hillside where many could sit on the grass and listen to him as he faced the hill.

Men and women argued for and against sexual freedom, religion, revolution, communism, anarchy, birth control, abortion, homosexuality, and police brutality. Some of the best speakers were hoboes or former hoboes. Ben Reitman always gathered a large crowd because he usually spoke about sexual matters. As each speaker finished, the custom was to pass the hat. A great speaker, like the legendary "King of the Soapboxers," John Loughman, could collect as much as thirty dollars while lesser speakers might only be able to gather a dollar or two.

As popular as Bughouse Square and the Hobo College was the Dil Pickle club, founded by Jack Jones, a former Wobbly who had fought in many strikes and free speech battles. He was rumored to be a saboteur, who had lost part of his right hand when a bomb he was planting exploded too soon. Jones had retired from his hobo/union life but still yearned for the company of his former companions. He opened a small coffee shop that he moved near Bughouse Square in 1916. It attracted a cross section of Chicago's intellectuals and underworld—providing a space where the hoboes, bums, tramps, prostitutes, pimps, gangsters, confidence men, labor leaders, lawyers, novelists, poets, and play-wrights met and mingled with each other and exchanged ideas. At that time, Chicago had some of the best novelists, poets, and journalists in America, including Carl Sandburg, Theodore Dreiser, Sherwood Anderson, Ring Lardner, Vachel Lindsay, Upton Sinclair, and Ben Hecht.

The Dil Pickle Club was once described as a place where the "inhabitants looked like bums and talked like college professors." It was in an alleyway; over the door hung a sign that read, "STEP HIGH . . . STOOP LOW . . . AND LEAVE YOUR DIGNITY OUTSIDE." Brundage described the club as a "dirty, dreary place where the smoke could be cut with a knife."

The Dil Pickle Club offered debates, plays, poems, music, and dances. It could hold 700 people and was usually jammed. The works of some of the world's best playwrights were performed by burlesque queens, prostitutes, and hoboes. Debates were held in which noted speakers argued with hoboes and tramps about everything from sexual practices to political philosophy to health diets. A number of famous professors and scientists lectured, on such subjects as insulin (which was new then) and how it was used to treat diabetes. One speaker was known as "Whispering Smith" because it was said his voice was so loud it could be heard at least four blocks away.

The Dil Pickle Club, like the Hobo College and Bughouse Square, began to fade and change by the 1930s. The world of the hobo and the tramp was coming to an end. The factors that gave birth to it—the railroad and the need for migrant manual labor in seasonal jobs—were no longer the same. Two events had happened by the end of the 1920s that marked the end of the hobo world: the development of the automobile and the onset of the Great Depression.

8

The End of the Road

You wonder why I'm a hobo and sleep in a ditch.
Well, it's not because I'm lazy, I just don't want to be rich. . . .

Now I could be a banker if I wanted to be.
But the thought of an iron cage is too suggestive to me.
Now I could be a broker without the slightest excuse.
But look at 1929 and tell me what's the use?

— TRADITIONAL HOBO VERSE

In 1921, a hobo by the name of Bill Quirke applied for a job at a packinghouse in Yakima, Washington, a job he was confident of getting. He was told that while there were jobs, the foreman had been ordered not to hire "floaters"—hoboes. They had been replaced by "the home guard"—local people, many of whom could drive to and from work in their own cars.

The 1920s saw the rise of the "rubber tramp," the migrant worker who owned his own car. The Pacific Rural Press had commented as early as 1923: "The automobile has created a new class of fruit workers." Henry Ford had made automobiles cheap enough for most people to buy, and a man who could scrape up $50 or so and knew something about mechanics could get a used "tin lizzie," as cars were called in those days. In it he could pack all his cooking and camping gear.

As the automobile replaced the railroad as the major means of transportation, machines replaced manual labor. By the 1920s, new

IN MEMORIAM

JOHN BARLEYCORN

BORN B.C.

DIED JAN. 16, 1920

RESURRECTION?

■ ONE EVENT THAT HELPED BRING THE HOBO ERA TO A CLOSE WAS PROHIBITION. IT MEANT THE END OF CHEAP DRINKS AND FREE LUNCHES. (*Courtesy of the Library of Congress*)

equipment made it possible for employers to hire far fewer men than before. Three men with a machine could now do the work once done by fifteen. A hobo in Chicago in 1922, looking at the jobs offered by the slave markets, wondered why there were so few jobs in many areas that traditionally needed workers. Hoboes who looked for jobs in lumber camps and wheat fields saw that they were far fewer than before World War I. Many began to take jobs they had once despised, like dishwashing or ditchdigging, because there was little else available. Other hoboes began to gravitate toward cities where, during the boom period of the 1920s, certain industries had a great need for labor.

There were other signs of the end of the hobo era as well. Prohibition had become the law of the land and the "Main Stem" of Chicago had changed dramatically. The saloons and the barrelhouses were gone. Speakeasies, where illegal liquor was served, didn't admit tramps and hoboes. The flophouses and the cheap restaurants, secondhand clothing stores, and missions survived, but everything else was changing. Many of the old-timers were aware that their way of life was over.

The final blow to the hobo world was the Great Depression. Until 1929, there were still some jobs for hoboes even though the number of men on the road seemed to be decreasing. When the Depression struck, the jobs vanished, but suddenly millions of unemployed men and women took to the road. Businessmen and factory workers, lawyers and college students, farmers and teachers joined the ranks of the hobo world. By 1933, over 16 million men and women—almost a third of the labor force—were out of work. Just as in previous depressions, millions of men and a smaller number of women and teenagers took to the road in search of work. One of them was seventeen-year-old Bill Bailey:

> There was very little food for the family and my mother was always worrying about where the food was coming from next . . . and I felt a humiliation that I was sitting down at the table and taking food out of others' mouths. You never ate too much because you wanted everybody to have their share. So you were always hungry. So by taking off and

■ DURING THE DEPRESSION, MANY HOMELESS PEOPLE LIVED IN MAKESHIFT SHACKS THEY BUILT FROM WASTE MATERIAL. *(Courtesy of the Library of Congress)*

going West, you felt that you had a chance to do something for the family. At least, there was one less mouth to feed.

Many teenagers who took off were looking for work and ways to support themselves and their families. But if they were unable to find work, as Bill was, then life on the road became an end in itself.

> I went to get a job on a ship in New York. And to get a job, you went up to the captain or a mate and you held your hat in your hand and you said, "Please captain, I can do anything. I'm a hard worker, I don't mind long hours and I don't make any trouble." By that you meant you weren't a union man. But since there wasn't any jobs to be had, I wound up bumming around the country. I became a hobo, although I always looked for work. So eventually, I began to ride the rails, jumping into boxcars. And they were filled with people. Thousands of them. Farmers, workers, people from all over—all of them like you were, going somewhere, looking for work. It was pretty obvious that most of them had been hard working people. You could see it just by looking at them. There were whole families riding together, mother, father, couple of kids in their rags, laying in the car, with runny noses, crying. There was nothing for them at home so they left. Boys and girls, some as young as 12. It was sad, but that's the way it was.

Bill was one of an estimated 200,000 teenage hoboes wandering across America. They came together in boxcars or jails, mission houses or jungles, and banded together for protection and friendship.

Like the hoboes of earlier generations, the road kids took to the trains. Thousands of them were killed or injured trying to do so. For one railroad alone, the Missouri Pacific, the overall statistics for death and injuries during the first four years of the Depression were grim: In 1929, 103 people killed, 156 injured; in 1930, 114 killed, 221 injured; in 1931, 125 killed and 247 injured; in 1932, 91 killed and 214 injured. Overall, 433 people were killed and 838 injured.

The road kids of the 1930s had left nothing behind them and had little to look forward to. Their one concern was survival. They were poorly clothed and underfed; they lived by their wits. Most of their

■ A YOUNG ROAD KID OF THE GREAT DEPRESSION "FLIPPING" A TRAIN. *(From Thomas Minehan's* Boy and Girl Tramps of America, *New York: Farrar and Rinehart, 1934)*

time was spent carrying the banner on the Main Stem for food, money, and alcohol. When they couldn't get anything, they stole—milk from doorsteps, groceries from vegetable trucks, purses from ladies, fruit from grocery stores. They admired big-time gangsters, but they themselves were, at best, petty thieves. They would walk as much as twenty miles in a day for food. Many turned to the mission houses, where they often had to sleep on the floor and eat peanut butter sandwiches, beef stew without the beef, and stale bread and doughnuts, washed down with dark water called coffee. Older men would grab food off young people's plates if they weren't careful, and many teenagers had to teach these men a lesson by beating them up or jabbing their wrist with a knife.

One major change that took place during the Great Depression was in the number of women on the road. Before 1929, there were very few women on the road. One study concluded that there was approximately one woman to every 200 hoboes and tramps before the Depression and one woman to twenty men after. Male hoboes generally did not think very highly of them. William Aspinwall, who spent most of his life wandering, recalled: "I have seen several women on the tramp but generally very low down creatures. The boys call them Bags, Old Bags." This was a limited view. There were women who lived a genuine hobo existence and were considered "road sisters." Some were extremely resourceful and made excellent hoboes. They decked trains and rode the blinds, rods, or reefers like any other hobo. When they needed money, they put on their one good dress, went into town and got a job—as a typist, file clerk, or house cleaner. One woman worked as a nurse. It wasn't always easy. Another woman who worked as a housekeeper found herself exploited, spending sixteen hours a day cooking, cleaning, sewing, washing, ironing, and taking care of ungrateful children. It was not surprising that many quit after they earned enough money to move on to the next location.

Many women on the road usually wore flannel shirts and coveralls to protect themselves from men. Sometimes, men's clothes served to disguise a woman as a young man. One woman dressed as a man worked her way across the Atlantic on a cattle ship. She smoked, drank, and chewed tobacco, and she cursed all the time. Only when she told her story to a newspaper after the voyage did the crew know that the young man was a woman.

However, many teenage girls had no skills other than domestic ones. They had left home for many of the same reasons as the boys: There were too many mouths to feed, bad relations with their parents, and the need to find work. Life in the road was more difficult for girls unless they had the protection of a boyfriend or a gang. Girls were under constant sexual pressure. Some exchanged sex with a brakeman for a ride on a train, or with a hobo for money or food. Another major problem was that the police and courts were much tougher on girls than on boys. A judge would tell a boy to get out of town, but put a girl in jail or send her to a reform school, usually charging her with being promiscuous. Sometimes a girl could persuade a policeman to let her go in exchange for sex.

Some road girls preferred to hitchhike rather than ride freights. They felt that men who owned cars were generally a better class of people than tramps that rode trains. It was fairly easy for a young girl to get a ride. It was also easier to control the situation. A man who had to keep his hands on the wheel of a car going forty miles an hour was far more manageable than a man or group of men sitting in a boxcar on a train and set on having sexual relations.

Anyone hitchhiking during the 1930s west of the Mississippi would have seen a new group of migrants on the road—not men traveling in groups and looking for seasonal jobs, but whole families packed in cars that should have been thrown on the scrap heap long ago. They were farmers from the Great Plains of America, from Oklahoma, Arizona, Arkansas, Texas, Colorado, Kansas, and Missouri. They had been wiped out by the falling prices of crops and by nature itself. As one farmer commented, "We were burned out, blown out, eaten out." In the early 1930s, a drought began that lasted through the decade. The land had been so badly misused that it turned to dust. In turn, the dust was caught up by the winds and carried in great storms that buried land, homes, cattle, and people's dreams. These "black blizzards," as they were called, turned day into night. One Oklahoma farm woman, Viola Cooper, recalled in an interview the day that the first blizzard struck:

> It started out to be a real beautiful spring day. It was mild and pleasant. Suddenly it began to get colder and colder. The temperature must of

dropped thirty or forty degrees in a few hours. Birds were everywhere. They came flying in from the North and whirled around like they was crazy, twittering and shaking—they just wouldn't stay still. You couldn't see anything wrong in the sky, but you just felt something awful was going to happen. Just as we was getting near our house, we saw it. It looked like one of them tidal waves rolling in clear up to the top of the sky. At first, we thought it was a big old snow blizzard except it was black. We called it a black blizzard. It was just dirt way high in the air. It looked like the clouds had fallen to the ground. It was pitiful. And when it hit the houses, no one could get their breath. You couldn't see a window in the house.

It was a good thing we was close to home or we never would have made it. The dirt was so thick we couldn't see the radiator cap on the truck. If you walked in front of it, you couldn't tell that the headlights was on unless you put your face right next to them. People got lost in that blizzard and were buried in it. Children died. They'd get lost from their parents and wander around in circles rather than stay in one place until someone found them. This one little boy I heard about got himself stuck on a barbed wire fence, couldn't get loose and was buried over by the dirt. We tried to protect ourselves as best we could. People put wet clothes over themselves and the kids. But it was hard to protect anybody from that dirt.

The blizzards, the dust, and the plague of grasshoppers that followed them drove people off their farms and onto the highways. Farm families became migrant families. They had read or heard that there were jobs in California and they headed west seeking work, like moths attracted to a flame. California held all the promises of paradise and the chance to start over again. Unlike hoboes and tramps, these migrants wanted to settle down. They were not wanderers by nature. Nor were they loners. They usually traveled together as a family; sometimes as many as six or seven people were packed in a car. Carey Mc-Williams, a journalist who wrote about the workers of the California fields, described them in the book *Farmers in the Field:*

> It is an army that marches from crop to crop. Its equipment is negligible, a few pots and pans. . . . It is supported by a vast horde of camp followers,

■ A GROUP OF "RUBBER TRAMPS" LOOKING FOR WORK SUFFER A BREAKDOWN ON THE ROAD. *(Courtesy of the Library of Congress)*

mostly pregnant women, diseased children and flea-bitten dogs. Its transport consists of a fleet of ancient and battered Model T Fords. . . . It has had many savage encounters with drought, floods and disease; and . . . its casualties have been heavy.

At first, the fruit and vegetable growers in California welcomed the migrants because they were cheap labor. A dollar a day for adults was the going rate, fifty cents or less for children. The migrants were also uncomplaining; they avoided strikes and worked together as a family in the fields. But as they flooded California by the hundreds of thousands,

■ A MIGRANT FAMILY ON THE ROAD TRAVELING FROM FARM TO FARM SEEKING EMPLOYMENT. (*Courtesy of the Library of Congress*)

the state turned hostile. The city of Los Angeles alone received 13 percent of the transients, providing aid for some 200,000. In response, the Los Angeles police began to patrol the California border hundreds of miles away. They set up roadblocks on highways and illegally turned back migrants, whom they called "the bum brigade" and "tin can tourists." Those who got past the roadblocks were rounded up farther on and dumped on the other side of the state line. Migrants arriving on trains were not allowed off. When some refused to leave California, they were threatened with beatings.

But despite the barriers, many still made it through to work in the fields. The work was brutal and poorly paid; the working conditions were miserable. A family of prune pickers, for example, began their day at four in the morning. Prune plums grew in trees and had to be "shaken" to the ground to be picked. Work started before dawn, when the prunes were cold and easy to knock down. Then parents and their children would go together in the orchard and begin to pick the prunes off the ground. At first, the picking was fun — the prunes were hard and the early morning cool. But as the day became hotter, the prunes became stickier and the work harder. The tension was often too much for the children, who would fight and cry and wind up getting slapped or spanked. By the end of the day, the family was angry and exhausted. Their backs ached from bending over continually, and their hands were covered with sticky prune juice. For six days a week they did this, until the season ended and the next crop was ready for picking.

If the working conditions were bad, the living conditions were worse. Many families lived in shacks made from cardboard cartons, in tents made from burlap, or in lean-tos covered with old rugs. The growers charged a nickel a bucket for water, so many migrants drank and washed from irrigation ditches because they could not afford to buy water. In some counties, an average of two children a day died from diarrhea, typhoid fever, polio, and influenza. The migrants ate beans, fried dough, dandelion greens, and boiled potatoes. Few children went to school. Children as young as five worked in the fields. Even many of those who went to school were forced to spend at least part of the day working in the fields. A magazine article written in 1924, entitled "Little Gypsies of the Field," described how migratory life affected children: "It turns home life into a drifting gypsy existence. . . . These children have no fixed center. They are children of the crops. They are born in the crops. The crops condition their lives. . . . When one child was asked 'Where is your home?', the child replied 'Home? We're cotton pickers.' "

World War II, which finally improved the condition of migrant workers, also put the finishing touches on the end of the hobo way of life. The war brought jobs and better working conditions, and it further increased the mechanization of work that had begun in the nineteenth century. Most unskilled trades became totally obsolete. Nor was a worker completely without means if he could no longer work. Government programs had been set up by President Roosevelt to provide some financial security for people when they retired. If some men continued to roam after the war ended, it was because they were personally unable to adjust to the new world. Those who stayed on the road turned to hitchhiking, because many of the new trains were too difficult to ride. But the general desire of most was to get out. As one relatively young hobo expressed it: "I'd do anything to get off the road. I've seen enough of the country. One city is like another. If a guy gets to traveling around too much, he can get to be a bum and I don't want to be a bum."

9

Conclusion

I crept with lice that stayed for spite
I froze in "jungles" more than can be said.
Dogs tore my clothes, and in a woeful plight
At many a back door for my food I pled
Until I wished to God that I was dead . . .
On every side the world was all my foe
Threatening me with jibe and jeer and chains
Hard benches, cells, and woe on endless woe
And yet that life was sweet for all its pains.

—HARRY KEMP, HOBO POET

The hobo era ended by 1940. But in the 1950s, it had a revival of sorts in a different form. A group of young men and women, many of them college-educated writers and poets, began to take to the highways of America much as the hoboes once had. They hitchhiked back and forth across the country, but they were not seeking work. They were on a spiritual quest, a search for a vision of the self and the meaning of life.

The high priest of this movement was Jack Kerouac. The book that made him famous was entitled *On the Road*. Kerouac expressed the theme of the book in his journal: "We follow the turn of the road and it leads us on. Where? To actuality. Ourselves! Others! God!"

The road symbolized a classic story that has appeared and reappeared since the earliest days of human literature. The hero of this story—unable to live in his homeland, usually for spiritual reasons—

takes to the road. Traveling, he has many wonderful and dangerous adventures, survives them, and becomes spiritually enlightened as a result of his experience. The hero's enlightenment enables him to return home with a message of salvation to all who will listen.

Kerouac's romantic vision of life on the road was expressed by others who wrote of the road during the heyday of the hobo. To those who idealized them, hoboes and tramps were the last of the rugged individualists, men who despised the capitalistic system and its corruption of values and exploitation of workers. They were spiritually pure, united by belonging to a brotherhood of outcasts.

But the reality of the hobo world was often far different from the dream existence that Kerouac envisioned. The world of hoboes and tramps was brutal and vicious; survival depended upon courage and wits. It was a life in which a man might go days without food, weeks without a decent place to sleep, and months without adequate clothing. It was an endless, repetitive, often meaningless existence. Jack London, who chose tramp life as a teenager, saw it for what it was: "I became a tramp begging my way from door to door, wandering over the United States and sweating my sweats in bloody prisons. I was in the pit, the abyss, the human cesspool, the schools and charnel house of our civilization. This is the part that society chooses to ignore."

But despite the hardships, some tramps found a deep satisfaction in their days on the road. They remembered the friendships they made, the adventures they had, the battles they fought and usually lost. One of those who expressed this point of view best was Harry Kemp. At the age of twelve, Harry began to work in a factory; he immediately knew that such a life was not for him. By the time he was sixteen, he was working on board a cattle ship bound for Australia. Later, he turned up in China. Then he traveled across America with a volume of poetry in his pocket, writing poems as he went, about the hardships and beauty of tramping. He loved life on the road and boasted about it to reporters years later when he had become somewhat famous: "Freedom is the one God I worship," he told one interviewer. To another he said,

"The tramp's greatest pleasure was to vanish like smoke . . . to shout and sing for the sheer happiness of freedom from responsibility and regular work."

Every hobo and tramp dreamed of a better life. This dream appeared in their poetry, songs, speeches, and letters. Perhaps nothing expresses it better than the most famous hobo ballad of all, in which, after years of traveling, a fictional hobo called Iowa Slim finally reaches the hoboes' paradise known as "The Big Rock Candy Mountains."

Where the ham and eggs grow on trees
And bread grows from the ground
And the springs spurt booze to your knees
And there's more than enough to go around

Where the chickens crawl into the skillet
And cook themselves up nice and brown
And the cows churn their butter in the mornin'
And squirt their milk all around.

Where the lunches grow on the bushes
And bump the 'boes in the eyes
And every night at eleven
The sky rains down apple pies.

His home is where the birds sing
And young girls swim in the fountains
And the cigarettes grow with the matches
In the big potato mountains.

In the Big Rock Candy Mountains
You never change your socks
And little streams of alcohol
Came a-trickling down the rocks
The boxcars are all empty
And the railroad bulls are blind
There's a lake of stew and whiskey too
You can paddle all around 'em in a big canoe
In the Big Rock Candy Mountains.

10

Epilogue: Hoboes and the Homeless

The question is sometimes raised whether there is any connection between the homeless of today and the hoboes of the past. There are more differences than similarities. Few homeless Americans today wander in search of work. When people are unemployed and need jobs, they usually remain in their own community. Social Security, unemployment insurance, Medicaid, and welfare, none of which existed during the days of migratory labor, now provide an economic safety net for many people.

In addition, there is far less demand for seasonal labor than there once was. Machinery has replaced manual labor in most industries, and many men who work in industries—such as mining and logging—that traditionally hired migrant labor now have high rates of unemployment. Nor is there any cheap means of getting to those jobs. There are fewer trains to flip, and few drivers will pick up hitchhikers' today.

Some homeless people are mentally ill. Many have serious problems with drugs and alcohol. They spend most of their time panhandling money to support their addiction. In this respect, they are like bums whose lives revolve around begging for money to buy alcohol.

Large numbers of women are homeless today. While we do not know how many homeless women there were in the past, we do know that relatively few women traveled. It may be that the numbers of homeless women have not greatly increased but that they are more visible than they were before. When the family broke down in the past, many women who could not find jobs to support themselves ended up

■ TODAY'S HOMELESS HAVE SOME THINGS IN COMMON WITH HOBOES AND TRAMPS. THEY TOO SUFFER FROM BEING MARGINAL PEOPLE IN A SOCIETY THAT HAS LITTLE PRODUCTIVE USE FOR THEM. *(Courtesy of the Library of Congress)*

in the streets as prostitutes or beggars, or in charitable institutions or jails.

Despite the many differences, there are a few similarities between the hoboes and tramps of the past and the homeless of today. The homeless do form temporary communities in public spaces, setting up "jungles" in parks, streets, and alleyways. Many panhandle to support themselves. There are criminals among the homeless just as once criminals were part of the tramp world.

One basic similarity is that many of the homeless are "marginal" people—that is, people who have the most difficulty finding work in the society. Like the hoboes of the past, many are unskilled and can find jobs only at the lower end of the economic ladder. These jobs are often short-term, and they do not pay enough to support a family. There is also fierce competition for these jobs from illegal immigrants, many of whom cannot work elsewhere.

Another major similarity is that hoboes and the homeless are both products of a society that does not provide sufficient jobs to enable men and women to support themselves and their families. Today, the economy of the United States is losing many well-paying jobs without creating enough new ones. This in turn creates the conditions that make people homeless—as it once created the conditions that made people hoboes. The tragedy is that those who do not learn from history are bound to repeat it.

A HOBO DICTIONARY

alki:	alcoholic
angel food:	mission sermon
batter:	to beg
bindle stiff:	hobo who carries a bundle usually containing shirts, socks, razor, etc.
blind, blind baggage:	space between the engine and the mail or baggage car
boomer:	seasonal or migratory
bridge snake:	structural iron worker
cannonball:	fast freight train; also called a dicer
carry the banner:	walk the streets all night
dingbat:	old hobo who mooches off other hoboes
dip:	pickpocket
flip:	hop a train
flop:	place to sleep
gandy dancer:	manual laborer on the railroad
gay cat:	tenderfoot hobo
glims:	spectacles, light
gump:	chicken
grinder:	teeth
harness bull:	policeman
hog:	locomotive
jackrolling:	robbing a drunk
java:	coffee
jolt:	jail sentence
jocker:	road kid's teacher and companion; the relationship is often sexual
jungle:	hobo camp
jungle buzzard:	tramp who hangs around jungles and begs
kicks:	shoes
lump:	handout
mark:	hobo sign indicating a person or institution willing to give food
mooch:	beg, usually at back doors

Mulligan stew:	hobo stew
mushfakir:	umbrella mender
panhandle:	beg
pearl diver:	dishwasher
profesh:	experienced hobo, sometimes a criminal
prushin:	young boy on the road
punk:	young hobo; also, bread
railroad bull:	railroad policeman
railroad dick:	railroad policeman
rattler:	train
road kid:	young hobo
shack:	brakeman
sky pilot:	mission-house preacher
slave market:	employment agency
stem:	street
stew bum:	old hobo wasted by alcohol
stiff:	any kind of hobo worker
town clowns:	town police
vag:	vagabond
wobs:	Wobblies, members of the I.W.W.
wolf:	older hobo who preys on young hoboes
yeggs:	criminals on the road, usually burglars and safecrackers

HOBO SIGNS

○—	Turn Right
—○	Turn Left
♂	Straight Ahead
� with teeth	A comb has teeth— So has a dog
⊓	Top Hat
♀ ∧∧	Kind Woman

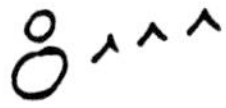

BIBLIOGRAPHY

Introduction

Allsop, Kenneth. *Hard Travellin': The Hobo and His History*. New York: New American Library, 1967.

Monkkonen, Eric. *Walking to Work: Tramps in America, 1790–1935*. Lincoln, Nebraska: University of Nebraska Press, 1984.

1. The "Bindle Stiff": The Hobo Worker

Armitage, Susan, and Elizabeth Jameson. *The Women's West*. Norman, Okla., and London: University of Oklahoma, 1987.

Bruns, Roger. *Knights of the Road: A Hobo History*. New York: Methuen, 1980.

Crampton, Frank. *Deep Enough: A Working Stiff in the Western Miners' Camp*. Denver: Sage Books, 1956.

Jensen, Vernon. *Lumber and Labor*. New York: Farrar and Rinehart, 1945.

Paul, Rodman W. *The Far West and the Great Plains in Transition, 1859–1900*. Harper and Row: New York, 1988.

White, Richard. *It's Your Misfortune and None of My Own*. Norman, Okla., and London: University of Oklahoma Press, 1991.

Wyman, Mark. *Hard Rock Epic: Western Miners and Industrial Revolution 1860–1910*. Berkeley: University of California, 1979.

2. Flipping Freights

Allsop, Kenneth. *Hard Travellin': The Hobo and His History*. New York: New American Library, 1967.

Bruns, Roger. *Knights of the Road: A Hobo History*. New York: Methuen, 1980.

Davies, William. *The Autobiography of a Super Tramp*. New York: Knopf, 1917.

Etulain, Richard, ed. *Jack London: On the Road*. Logan, Utah: Utah State University Press, 1979.

Lynn, Ethel. *The Adventures of a Woman Hobo.* New York: George Doran, 1917.

Willard Flynt, Josiah. *Tramping with Tramps: Studies and Sketches of Vagabond Life.* New York: Century Company, 1899.

Tully, Jim. *Beggars of Life.* New York: Albert and Charles Boni, 1924.

3. "Vampires of the Road": Tramps

Allsop, Kenneth. *Hard Travellin': The Hobo and His History.* New York: New American Library, 1967.

Bruns, Roger. *Knights of the Road: A Hobo History.* New York: Methuen, 1980.

Davies, William. *The Autobiography of a Super Tramp.* New York: Knopf, 1917.

Etulain, Richard, ed. *Jack London: On the Road.* Logan, Utah: Utah State University Press, 1979.

Willard Flynt, Josiah. *Tramping with Tramps: Studies and Sketches of Vagabond Life.* New York: Century Company, 1899.

Milburn, George. *The Hobo's Handbook.* New York: Iven, Wrinkling, 1930.

Reitman, Ben. *Sister of the Road.* New York: Macauley, 1937.

4. Road Kids

London, Jack. *The Road.* New York: Macmillan, 1907.

Tully, Jim. *Beggars of Life.* New York: Albert and Charles Boni, 1924.

5. Terrors and Tragedies of the Road

Allsop, Kenneth. *Hard Travellin': The Hobo and His History.* New York: New American Library, 1967.

Kemp, Harry. *Tramping on Life.* New York: Garden City Press, 1927.

Pinkerton, Allan. *Strikers, Communists, Tramps, and Detectives.* New York: Trows, 1878.

6. The Wobblies

Dubofsky, Melvyn. *We Shall Be All: A History of the Industrial Workers of the World.* Urbana, Ill.: University of Illinois, 1968, 1986.

Haywood, Bill. *The Autobiography of Big Bill Haywood.* New York: International Publishers, 1974.

Kornbuth, Joyce L., ed. *Rebel Voices: An I.W.W. Anthology.* Ann Arbor, Mich.: University of Michigan Press, 1964.

Renshaw, Patrick. *The Wobblies.* New York: Anchor, 1968.

Schwantes, Carlos. *Coxey's Army: An American Odyssey.* Lincoln, Neb.: University of Nebraska, 1985.

7. Chicago: Hobo Capital of the World

Bruns, Roger. *The Damnedest Radical: The Life and World of Ben Reitman, Chicago's Celebrated Social Reformer, Hobo King and Whorehouse Physician.* Urbana and Chicago: University of Illinois Press, 1987.

Cronon, William. *Nature's Metropolis: Chicago and the Great West.* New York and London: W. W. Norton, 1991.

Duis, Perry R. *The Saloon: Public Drinking in Chicago and Boston, 1880–1920.* Urbana and Chicago: University of Illinois Press, 1983.

8. The End of the Road

Hurt, Douglas R. *The Dust Bowl: An Agricultural and Social History.* Chicago: Nelson-Hall, 1981.

Kromer, Tom. *Waiting for Nothing.* New York: Knopf, 1931.

McWilliams, Carey. *Farmers in the Field.* Hamden, Conn.: Archon, 1969.

Minehan, Thomas. *Boy and Girl Tramps of America.* New York: Farrar and Rinehart, 1934.

Stein, Walter J. *California and the Dust Bowl Migration.* Westport, Conn.: Greenwood, 1973.

9. Conclusion

Kemp, Harry. *Tramping on Life.* New York: Garden City Press, 1927.

Kerouac, Jack. *On the Road.* New York: Penguin, 1976.

INDEX

Page numbers in italics refer to illustrations.